CATHOLIC MISSIONARY HEROES

VOLUME I

Father Robert J. Kus

Wilmington, North Carolina

www.redlanternpress.com

Publications of Red Lantern Press

Journals by Fr. Robert J. Kus

- Dreams for the Vineyard: Journal of a Parish Priest - 2002
- For Where Your Treasure Is: Journal of a Parish Priest – 2003
- There Will Your Heart Be Also: Journal of a Parish Priest – 2004
- Field of Plenty: Journal of a Parish Priest – 2005
- Called to the Coast: Journal of a Parish Priest – 2006
- Llamado a la Costa - Diario de un párroco – 2006
- Then Along Came Marcelino: Journal of a Parish Priest – 2007
- Y Después Llegó Marcelino - Diario de un párroco – 2007
- Living the Dream: Journal of a Parish Priest – 2008
- Viviendo el Sueño: Diario de un Párroco - 2008
- A Hand to Honduras: Journal of a Parish Priest – 2009
- Una Mano a Honduras: Diario de un Párroco - 2009
- Beacon of Hope: Journal of a Parish Priest – 2010
- Luz de Esperanza: Diario de un Párroco - 2010
- Serving God by Serving Others: Journal of a Parish Priest – 2011
- Servir a Dios Sirviendo a Los Demás: Diario de un Párroco – 2011
- The Year of Clifton: Journal of a Parish Priest – 2012
- Basilica: Journal of a Parish Priest – 2013
- Crucifix: Journal of a Parish Priest – 2014
- Holy Doors: Journal of a Parish Priest – 2015
- Amazing!: Journal of a Parish Priest – 2016
- Clear and Misty: Journal of a Parish Priest – 2017
- Honduras Calling: Journal of a Missionary Priest – 2018
- Home in Honduras: Journal of a Missionary Priest – 2019
- MissionPriest.com: Journal of a Missionary Priest – 2020
- Hormiga Junction: Journal of a Missionary Priest – 2021

Publications of Red Lantern Press (Cont.)

Reitocan Books by Fr. Robert J. Kus

- Reitocan Grace – Gracia Reitoqueña: A Honduran Parish in Photos and Scripture
- Reitocan Faith – Fe Reitoqueña: A Honduran Parish in Photos and Scripture
- Reitocan Joy – Alegria Reitoqueña : A Honduran Parish in Photos and Scripture

Homily Collections by Fr. Robert J. Kus

- Flowers in the Wind 1 – Story-Based Homilies for Cycle B
- Flowers in the Wind 2 – Story-Based Homilies for Cycle C
- Flowers in the Wind 3 – Story-Based Homilies for Cycle A
- Flowers in the Wind 4 – More Story-Based Homilies for Cycle A
- Flowers in the Wind 5 – More Story-Based Homilies for Cycle B
- Flowers in the Wind 6 – More Story-Based Homilies for Cycle C
- Flowers in the Wind 10 – Even More Story-Based Homilies for Cycle A
- Flowers in the Wind 11 – Even More Story-Based Homilies for Cycle B
- Flowers in the Wind 12 – Even More Story-Based Homilies for Cycle C

Nursing and Saints by Fr. Robert J. Kus

- Saintly Men of Nursing: 100 Amazing Stories
- Hombres Santos de la Enfermería: Cien Historias Asombrosas

Catholic Missionary Heroes Collection by Fr. Robert J. Kus

- Catholic Missionary Heroes – Volume 1

Dedication

To

Pope Francis

A True Servant-Leader

Acknowledgments

Writing the biographies presented in this book was possible only because of the work of many others, most of whom will never be known to me. They are, for example, the hidden writers of websites such as Wikipedia and those of religious communities who never sign their names to their works. To those folks, and for all who write about Catholic heroes, I give my heartfelt thanks!

I also give special thanks to my friend, Dr. Aaron Mejía, who has been with me every step of the way in creating and editing the MissionPriest.com website from its beginning.

I thank Pat Marriott of the Basilica Shrine of St. Mary in Wilmington, North Carolina, who has faithfully edited my work throughout the years and encouraged me on life's path.

And finally, I thank you, dear readers. I hope the Spirit speaks to you through the stories of these fine men and women, inspiring you on your own spiritual journeys.

The Cover

The front cover of this book, a painting by artist Alessandro Giambra, shows six of the 35 Catholic missionary heroes featured in this book. The six are, from top right clockwise: Father Bill Woods, Blessed Carlo Acutis, Mother Mary Joseph Rogers, Blessed James Miller, Ms. Jean Donovan, and Ms. Annalena Tonelli.

Alessandro Giambra, originally from Italy, teaches Italian, art theory and painting in the St. Mary Adult School on the campus of the Basilica Shrine of St. Mary, Wilmington, North Carolina.

Introduction

On April 26, 2020, the first post of my blog and website, MissionPriest.com, appeared online. The primary purpose of the blog is to share my life as a missionary priest with others who would like know more about missionary life in another country, yet are unable to have this experience directly.

On most Fridays, the site provides a short biography of a "Catholic missionary hero." This book is a collection of the men and women heroes who have appeared on the MissionPriest.com website during the year 2020. The plan is to add a new volume every year as long as the website continues. I alternate men and women heroes each week.

Though there are noble missionary heroes in other Christian traditions, such as Protestantism (including evangelicalism) and Orthodox Christianity, this series focuses exclusively on Catholic heroes.

The purpose of this book is to introduce readers to mission heroes and whet their appetites. It is not meant to be a scholarly investigation. Hopefully, these short biographical sketches will pique the interest of readers, and they will be tempted to learn more.

At the end of the book, I provide a selected bibliography to provide readers with a place to begin further exploration.

Many of the people in this collection have been canonized, and are thus known as "Saint," or they are on the official path to sainthood and have the title "Servant of God," "Venerable," or "Blessed."

Some people have more than one name. In some religious communities, for example, members take new names in religious life. For example, pretty much everyone has heard of "Saint Teresa of Calcutta," but they might not have heard of Agnes Gonxha Bojaxhiu, who is the same person.

I hope you enjoy this volume of Catholic Missionary Heroes as much as I have enjoyed creating it!

Fr. Robert J. Kus
Reitoca, F.M., Honduras
Missionpriest.com
September 2022

Table of Contents

CATHOLIC MISSIONARY HEROES

VOLUME I

1
Ms. Annalena Tonelli
April 2, 1943 – October 5, 2003
The Mother Teresa of Somalia

Annalena Tonelli was born on April 2, 1943, in Forli, Italy. As a young adult, she became a lawyer specializing in legal services for those of her town in most need – the poor, orphans, the mentally ill, the disabled, and abused children.

In 1969, as a young woman, Annalena went to Kenya, sponsored by the Committee Against World Hunger of Forli.

In Kenya, Annalena began working as a teacher in a secondary school in the area of Wajir, but after some years, she decided to enter nursing school. As a nurse, she worked more than a decade caring for those most in need in Kenya.

In 1976, Annalena led a pilot project for the World Health Organization, demonstrating methods for treating tuberculosis in nomadic peoples. To ensure that the patients would take their medications faithfully over a treatment course of six months, Annalena invited the nomadic tuberculosis patients to come to the Rehabilitation Center for the Disabled that she operated with the help of other women volunteers. The pilot project was a success, and the World Health Organization adopted this model for other areas of the world.

Annalena also created a school for the deaf in Wajir. Many of the graduates of this school went on to start schools in Somali-speaking Africa, and it was in this school that Somali Sign Language was first used.

In 1984, the Kenyan army engaged in the massacre of 5,000 Somali boys and men. Annalena and her volunteers followed the trail of blood to collect the bodies of the dead and treat wounded survivors. Annalena brought with her a photographer to document this male genocide. From that moment on, she was seen as an enemy of the Kenyan government and was banned from the country.

From Kenya, Annalena moved to Somalia, where she stayed for the next 19 years. During this time, she started a tuberculosis hospital, and persuaded her family and friends in Italy to help finance the hospital by contributing money each month to maintain it.

In June of 2003, the United Nations High Commissioner for Refugees awarded Annalena Tonelli the Nansen Refugee Award. This prize is given annually to recognize outstanding service to the cause of refugees. On October 5, 2003, just four months after Annalena received her international award, one or more gunmen assassinated Annalena at her tuberculosis hospital. Two weeks after Annalena Tonelli's killing, two other workers were murdered in Somalia at their school. Many believe the assassins were members of the same group that assassinated Annalena.

There are many theories about these assassinations. Some say it was because Annalena brought HIV/AIDS patients to the area. Others felt she was spreading disease in the town. Others said that the killer was a disgruntled former worker who had been fired. And others said it was a radical Islamic terrorist group that wanted her dead.

2
Saint Anthony of Padua, O.F.M.
ca. 1195 – June 13, 1231
He Showed Them How to Preach!

Fernando Martins de Bulhões was born around 1195 in Lisbon, Portugal into a wealthy family. Although his family wanted him to live as a noble, Fernando chose instead to become an Augustinian friar.

After ordination as a priest of his order, Fr. Fernando was put in charge of hospitality in his abbey. One day in 1219, he welcomed five Franciscan friars who were on their way to Morocco as missionaries to preach to Muslims there. Not long after this encounter, Fernando learned that all five of the Franciscans had been martyred in Morocco.

Impressed by the simplicity of the Franciscans' lifestyle, and intrigued by their martyrdom, in 1220, Francisco entered the Franciscan order and took the name Anthony.

Soon, he traveled as a missionary to Morocco with another friar. Unfortunately, he became ill and had to return home. However, on the way home to Portugal, he was shipwrecked and landed in Sicily. From there, he traveled to Italy where he would spend the rest of his life. He joined a Franciscan community in Padua, where he served in the kitchen.

One day, Fr. Anthony had an experience that changed the direction of his life. On that day, his house was to host an ordination, and many Dominican friars were invited. The Dominicans supposed a Franciscan would preach at the Mass since they were the hosts, and the Franciscans supposed a Dominican would preach since Dominicans like to think of themselves as great preachers.

When the Abbot learned that nobody was prepared to preach, he asked Anthony to be the homilist. When Anthony objected that he was unworthy to do so, he was told to simply listen to the Holy Spirit. So, that's what Anthony did. His preaching was so clear, and his style so simple yet captivating, that the assembly was spellbound.

After that, the Minister General of his order commissioned Fr. Anthony to preach the good news of Jesus throughout northern Italy. And, at times, he was even invited to teach at great universities in France.

Fr. Anthony of Padua died in 1231. Legend says that when he died, children cried in the streets, and angels came down from heaven to ring the bells of all the churches. Anthony of Padua was canonized in 1232 by Pope Gregory IX. His feast day is June 13.

St. Anthony of Padua is a patron saint of a wide variety of things. Though he is most famous for being the saint in charge of lost objects ("St. Anthony, St. Anthony, please look around, something is lost and now must be found!"), he is also the patron saint of such places as Beaumont, Texas; fishermen; the elderly; pregnant women; sailors; shipwrecks; and travelers. So, he has plenty to do to keep himself busy in heaven!

3
Saint Augustine of Canterbury, O.S.B.
Early 6th Century – probably May 26, 604
The Apostle of England

Just as St. Patrick is often called the Apostle of Ireland, and St. Boniface is called the Apostle of Germany, today's missionary hero – St. Augustine of Canterbury – is frequently called the Apostle of England. (St. Augustine of Canterbury should not be confused with the great African bishop, St. Augustine of Hippo.)

After his early education, Augustine became a Benedictine monk and was ordained to the priesthood. In time, Fr. Augustine became the prior of the Benedictine monastery in Rome. On the orders of Pope Gregory the Great,

Fr. Augustine and forty monks went from Rome to bring Christianity to the Anglo-Saxon people in what today is known as England.

When the missionary band arrived in Gaul (present-day France), they heard nightmarish tales of how ferocious the Anglo-Saxon people were and how dangerous it was to cross the English Channel. So, Augustine and his monks returned to Rome. Gregory, however, told them that the tales they had heard were groundless, and that they should go back.

So, Augustine and his men went to the southeastern part of England called Kent, which includes the present but much smaller County of Kent. It was ruled by a pagan named Ethelbert, who was married to a Christian woman. Ethelbert received the band of missionaries kindly, and soon they set up their headquarters in Canterbury. On Pentecost Sunday, 597, Augustine baptized King Ethelbert, along with many others.

Soon afterwards, Augustine was consecrated a bishop. He built a monastery in Canterbury and founded his see (diocese). (The historic cathedral of Canterbury was consecrated centuries later.) Eventually, Bishop Augustine also founded other dioceses including that of London, and he appointed several bishops to serve various parts of England.

St. Augustine of Canterbury died between 604 and 605. As the founder of Christianity in the British Isles, he is one of the favorite saints of England. His feast day is May 27.

4
Father Bill Woods, M.M.
September 14, 1931 - November 20, 1976
A Texas Cowboy for Jesus

A missionary hero and martyr of our times is Fr. Bill Woods.

Bill was born in Houston, Texas on September 14, 1931, and was ordained a Maryknoll Missionary priest in 1958. After his ordination, Fr. Bill was assigned to work in Barillas, a town in western Guatemala near the sparsely populated jungle regions of Ixcán, a municipality of Quiché.

Like many new Maryknoll missionaries, Fr. Bill came to his first assignment filled with all the hope, joy, and enthusiasm of a newly-ordained priest. Bishop John McCarthy, his close friend, said, "Fr. Bill was a Texas cowboy for Jesus, ready to enjoy the open spaces of Guatemala, to ride horses, jeeps, airplanes, and motorcycles, and to teach the Indians about the Catholic faith."

While in Barillas, Fr. Bill opened a wood-carving cooperative for about 25 poor indigenous families and a clinic. But Fr. Bill knew that he was called to make a difference on a much larger scale, notably to help poor people get their own land.

At that time, the Guatemalan government began a program allowing poor peasants to settle in the inhospitable Ixcán, a jungle near Barillas. This inspired Fr. Bill to develop a homesteading program in the Ixcán jungle, serviced by small airplanes, wherein the indigenous people would be flown into the jungle to carve out farms for themselves. Pilots could then fly their produce out of the jungles to local markets.

In 1965, Fr. Bill learned how to fly a plane and purchased 100 square miles of land between two rivers. He invited a lawyer to help with land titles and distributed equal-sized plots of land to the people. Rather than individual ownership, however, Fr. Bill made sure that the titles for the plots of land were registered in the name of the cooperatives he founded. That would make it impossible for the rich to buy out individual farms once the indigenous people had developed the land and made it profitable.

By 1975, ten years after Fr. Bill learned to fly, he had three small planes to service the five cooperatives he had founded. He and his pilot friends had flown over twelve thousand trips to and from the Ixcán. Approximately 2,000 families had been settled, forming five towns that operated as co-operative enterprises. Nurseries were set up, schools were built, and new plants were introduced. Over 1,000 head of cattle were being raised by the five cooperatives. Each town had a clinic with nurses and paramedics.

To meet the spiritual needs of the people, each cooperative had a chapel and meeting hall that was headed by *Delegados de la Palabra* (Delegates of the Word), lay ministers who performed administrative and certain spiritual services for small Catholic churches in Central American nations in the absence of a priest. The *Delegados* also helped catechists provide religious instruction.

In the early 1970s, oil prices began to rise, and the Guatemalan government was ready to start drilling. Guatemala's military leaders, favored by the rich and the dictatorial government, set their sights on taking over the land developed by Fr. Bill and the indigenous people he served. When the army came to capture the land, many of the people fled in fright. Fr. Bill, however, would not back down. He took the case to the government and fought for the poor. As a voice for the poor and powerless, he was labeled a troublemaker and marked for death.

Realizing that he was a target of the anti-indigenous forces, Fr. Bill once pointed to the sky over the jungle and said, "That is where they're going to get me one day."

On November 20, 1976, on a cloudless day, Fr. Bill flew a physician, an American journalist, a lay missionary, and one other person to visit a co-operative in the Ixcán. Just after 11 in the morning, on a perfectly clear day, the plane crashed into a mountain. In an instant, Guatemalan military units, who "just happened" to be in this remote jungle area, quickly removed key engine parts that would have proven the plane had been shot down.

Fr. Bill Woods and lay missioner John Gauker were buried with honors in Huehuetenango. Thousands of indigenous people attended their funeral.

5
Saint Boniface, O.S.B.
ca. 672 - 754
Apostle to Germany

An English priest with the inauspicious name of Winfred was grandly renamed Boniface by Pope Gregory II when he was commissioned for grand works.

Winfred was born in England around 672. Against his father's wishes, he became a Benedictine monk. In time, he went to the Germanic countries of northern Europe to see what he could do to spread the Christian faith. There, he found that although there were traces of Christianity, the people for the most part had lost the basics of the faith and intermingled their Christian beliefs with pagan ones.

He also discovered that priests there were lax in their religious observance, and many of them were not in harmony with their bishops. Part of the problem was, of course, a lack of education, a lack of discipline, a lack of easy communication, and a lack of solid leadership. So, Boniface tried to remedy the situation as best he could.

After being consecrated a bishop, Boniface established many monasteries in Germany and encouraged Religious Sisters to engage in education. In time, Germany became a leading light of the Christian faith in Europe, and Boniface is credited for being a unifier of Europe. He is regarded as the "Apostle to Germany."

Boniface died in 754 and is honored as a saint not only by Catholic Christians, but also by many Protestant and Orthodox Christians. His feast day is June 5.

6
Saint Camillus de Lellis, M.I.
May 25, 1550 – July 14, 1614
A Nurse Missionary

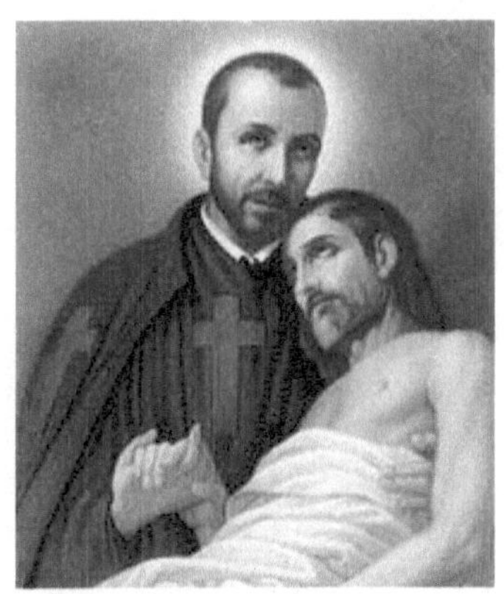

One of the greatest nurses of all time was Camillus de Lellis, an Italian who lived from 1550 to 1614. When he was 16, he became a soldier like his father. Camillus was a huge man, six feet six inches tall, and he had a fiery temper. As a soldier, he lived a wild lifestyle of drinking and brawling and getting into all kinds of trouble. His biggest problem, however, was his addiction to gambling.

When he was 21, Camillus was admitted to a hospital in Rome because of a spreading leg ulcer that would not heal. But his quarrelsome ways led to his dismissal from the hospital.

By the time he was 24, Camillus' gambling addiction had lost him everything he had ever owned, including the very shirt off his back. Reduced to a pauper, Camillus remembered a vow he had made earlier in life to become a Franciscan. The Franciscans took him in as a laborer, but they could not keep him because of his incurable leg ulcer.

Camillus returned to the hospital, and there he began an amazing transformation. He began to care for the sick as a nurse, and he became angry at the poor nursing care that was being done there. Therefore, he set out to make some changes. He was so spectacular as a nurse, and his changes were so successful that he eventually became the hospital administrator.

During Camillus' time at the hospital, he also studied for the priesthood, and was ordained when he was 34 years old.

Camillus founded his own hospital, and over time he assembled a group of men who had a similar devotion to serving God by serving others. These men eventually became known as the Ministers of the Sick (M.I.), priests and Brothers who served the sick physically and spiritually. The emblem of these men was a large red Latin cross, which they wore on their habits and on their capes.

Some of the Ministers of the Sick, who eventually came be known as the Camillian Fathers & Brothers, cared for plague victims. Many became infected by the plague and died. Others were sent to battlefields in Hungary and Croatia to care for the sick, where many died in battle. Camillus and his followers had a special love for prisoners, people suffering from the plague, and soldiers.

Camillus instituted many modern nursing practices such as proper ventilation, good nutrition, and isolation of patients with contagious diseases. Many of his principles are taught even today in schools of nursing and schools of medicine.

Camillus insisted that his priests and brothers see Christ in every sick person and insisted on what he called "old-fashioned charity with up-to-date technical skill." His guiding principle was the words of Jesus, "Whatever you did for one of these least brothers of mine, you did for me" (Mt 25: 40). By the time of his death, he had established fifteen houses of his congregation and eight hospitals.

The Order of St. Camillus continues his religious and healing tradition today, and many churches call their ministry to the sick the "Camillus ministry."

Camillus was canonized in 1746. Today, St. Camillus is a patron saint of nurses, nursing administrators, hospitals, and the sick. St. Camillus' feast day is July 18.

7
Sister Carla Piette, M.M.
September 29, 1939 - August 23, 1980
Servant of the Divine Circus Master

Carla Piette was a heroic woman who gave her life so that her friend could live.

When she was 19 years old and a student at Marquette University, Carla decided to become a Maryknoll Missionary Sister. Her superiors described her as "… friendly, outgoing, jovial, big-hearted and generous, but rather naïve and tactless."

Carla was also somewhat anti-clerical. She didn't care if a man was a priest or a bishop; she treated him as anyone else. But, as we will see, she did admire people who preached a Gospel of love, especially champions of the poor.

Carla served as a missionary in Chile from 1964 to 1979. During her time there, she worked with the poorest of the poor. Though she suffered from depression from time to time, her very strong inner core allowed her to serve God by serving others day after day. One of her biographers, Jacqueline Hansen Maggiore, described Carla as a "… teacher, parish leader, prophet, clown, poet and scripture scholar."

In 1973, Carla made friends with another Maryknoll Sister named Ita Ford. Carla and Ita were so close as friends and coworkers that people began calling them "Carla y Ita" – Carla and Ita – which in Spanish sounds like one word – "Carlita" or "Little Carla."

During these years, Chile experienced great turmoil. President Allende was killed, and soldiers filled the streets. Government death squads under dictator Augusto Pinochet killed tens of thousands of people. Over 300 Catholic missionaries and priests were ordered out of the country, and at least three were killed.

After serving in Chile, both Carla and Ita took a break. But back in the United States, they longed to serve the great needs of the people in Central and South American nations.

In 1980, Carla and Ita heard the call of an amazing man named Oscar Romero, the Archbishop of San Salvador. He called on Church workers from other nations to help the Church in El Salvador, which was experiencing incredible persecution.

Ominously, Sr. Carla arrived in El Salvador on the day Archbishop Romero was martyred, and Sr. Ita arrived in El Salvador on the day of his funeral. Little did they know that their time on earth was also soon coming to an end.

In El Salvador, they found themselves in the middle of a war, a war against the poor. They did their best to bury the dead, help priests escape, feed the poor, console those in sorrow, and serve refugees. Every day, both Sisters knew that they might be the next to lose their lives.

On August 22, 1980, Sr. Carla wrote to a friend, "We dolly along in this crazy circus of life where so often the Divine Circus Master doesn't clue us into the act for tomorrow yet always gives us the strength to perform … I leave the future in the Circus Master's hands."

One day later, on August 23, 1980, Sisters Carla and Ita escorted a man who had just been released from prison to his town. After delivering him, they were on their way back home when a flash flood submerged their car in water. Carla, who was big and strong, lifted the petite Ita and pushed her out of the window. Sr. Ita was miraculously saved, but Sr. Carla drowned. She gave her life for her friend.

Though Sr. Ita lived, we know that it was not for long. For on December 2, 1980, Maryknoll Sisters Ita Ford and Maura Clarke, along with two missionaries from Cleveland, Ohio – Ursuline Sister Dorothy Kazel and Lay Missionary Jean Donovan – were martyred for the faith: raped, shot, and buried in shallow graves for the crimes of being who they were and doing what they did for the people.

8
Blessed Carlo Acutis
May 3, 1991 - October 12, 2006
The Internet Missionary

Carlo Acutis was born on May 3, 1991 in London to Italian parents who were working there at the time. Soon after his birth, however, the family moved to Milan.

 After he received his First Communion at the age of seven, Carlo showed a strong religious spirit. He loved to attend Mass and receive Communion, and he had strong devotion to Jesus in the Blessed Sacrament. He also had special devotion to saints, especially Francis of Assisi, Francisco and Jacinta Marto, Dominic Savio, Tarcisius, Bernadette Soubirous, and Jesus' mother, Mary.

As a youngster, Carlo developed strong computer skills and devoted much of his time cataloging Eucharistic miracles that had been reported in the world. Those he put on a website he had developed. He also enjoyed film and comic editing. On his website, he wrote: "The more Eucharist we receive, the more we will become like Jesus, so that on this earth we will have a foretaste of heaven."

In his teens, Carlo was diagnosed with leukemia. He frequently went on pilgrimages with his parents to sites where Eucharistic miracles had been reported. One of his favorite places to visit was Assisi, Italy.

Carlo died on October 12, 2006 in Milan, and was buried in Assisi. On October 10, 2020, the Church beatified him in a beautiful ceremony in Assisi. He was displayed in a glass coffin wearing jeans and a pair of Nikes, the "habit" of computer programmers everywhere.

Carlo was a true missionary by spreading the good news of Jesus, not by physically traveling his country or visiting distant lands, but rather by using the gift of the Internet to spread the word.

Blessed Carlo Acutis is a patron of youth, students, the Internet, and computer programmers. His feast day is October 14.

9
Servant of God Casimir Cypher, O.F.M., Conv.
January 12, 1941 - June 25, 1975
Wisconsin Priest, Honduran Martyr

Michael Cypher, later known in Religious life as Fr. Casimir, was a missionary of our time who was killed for the faith.

Michael was born on January 12, 1941 in Medford, Wisconsin. He was the tenth of twelve children of a farm family.

After spending his childhood and teen years in Catholic schools, Michael joined the Conventual Franciscans. As a seminarian, Michael was known for his great kindness, sense of humor, simplicity, and generosity. He loved nature and loved to write.

He graduated from Loyola University in Chicago and was ordained a priest in 1968. In Religious life, he took the name of Casimir.

After serving as a parish priest in Illinois and California, Fr. Casimir felt called to the missions of Honduras. As a missionary, he went to the Department of Olancho. (A Honduran "department" is like an American or Mexican state.) There, he worked with the poorest of the poor. Public health at the time was sadly deficient: even in the general population, almost half of all children died before the age of five.

In the missions, Fr. Casimir celebrated Mass and other sacraments with the people, ran a parish and school, and served in any way he could. Though his Spanish was far from perfect, the people loved him because they knew he loved them.

During his time in Honduras, there was great political strife in the country. Though Fr. Casimir was not known for being political, as a Catholic priest he was seen by the government as a champion of the poor and thus an enemy.

On June 25, 1975, five thousand poor and landless peasants began a six-day "Hunger March" from Olancho to the nation's capital, Tegucigalpa, to demand that the government act on its promises for land reforms.

Paramilitary groups controlled by wealthy landowners, and the Honduran Army, moved to stop the march, raided the bishop's residence, attacked Catholic rectories, and terrorized civil institutions associated with the reform movement.

On the day of the march, Fr. Casimir was taking an old truck to the repair shop. When he heard shots coming from the public square, he ran to see what was happening. Many believed that the soldiers mistook him for a particularly notorious priest, while others said that his identity didn't matter, as all priests were seen as enemies of the state.

Casimir was captured, stripped naked, and beaten. Despite constant humiliation from the authorities, he ran through the square blessing dead bodies of the poor and anointing those still alive. Finally, he, another priest, and some women were taken to a detention facility and sentenced to death. Many people were baked alive. After unspeakable torture, the priests were shot in the head. The priests' dead bodies were thrown into a dry well with live people, dynamited, and then bulldozed to conceal the crime. With the help of the United States government, the bodies were found and buried.

Fr. Casimir was only 34 years old when he was murdered for the faith. Today, people all over Honduras honor him in the Cathedral of Gualaco in Olancho.

Today, he is known as Servant of God Casimir Cypher, the first step on the journey to canonization.

10
Saint Damien of Molokai, SS.CC.
January 3, 1840 - April 15, 1889
The Leper Priest

Jozef De Veuster was the seventh child of a Flemish corn merchant and his wife on January 3, 1840 in Tremelo in Belgium. The faith of his family was quite strong. In fact, two of his sisters became Religious Sisters, and Jozef and his brother Auguste became priests.

Jozef had to quit school when he was thirteen to work on the family farm. When he was nineteen, he entered the Congregation of the Sacred Hearts of Jesus and Mary. In Religious life, he took the name Damien. His brother Auguste, known as Fr. Pamphile in Religious life, was also a member of this Order, which is often known as the Picpus congregation.

When Damien entered the Order on October 7, 1860, his superiors deemed him unsuitable for ordination because of his inadequate education. However, his brother tutored him, and eventually Damien was able to study for the priesthood. During his seminary studies, he prayed every day before a picture of the great missionary, St. Francis Xavier, that one day he would be given the honor of being a missionary.

Three years after entering the Picpus Order, Damien got his wish. When his brother Pamphile was unable to take a missionary assignment to Hawaii, Damien took his place.

On March 19, 1864, Damien landed in Honolulu harbor on the island of Oahu, and on May 21, 1864, he was ordained a priest.

Fr. Damien's first assignment was on the island of Hawaii, but in 1873, he volunteered to serve in the Hawaiian government's leper colony in Kalaupapa on the island of Molokai.

Initially, the plan was for four priests to serve on Molokai for three months each year. But when Fr. Damien went there, he fell in love with the people, the place, and the unlimited opportunities to do mission work. Molokai was a missionary's dream.

In those days, lepers were treated horribly. Once a person was diagnosed with leprosy, now known as Hansen's disease, he or she was taken to the island by boat and thrown overboard once the boat got close to the shore. The leper then had to swim to shore or drown.

When Fr. Damien first encountered the more than 800 lepers in the colony, he was appalled. The site of rotten toes and fingers and noses was horrifying, and the stench of the wounds was bad. However, Damien became used to the sights and smells, and soon he found himself nursing the sick as best he could. He also made coffins and dug graves when a member of his flock died.

Fr. Damien quickly realized that it fell to him to build structures for the people. Soon, with the people's help, he built new houses, an orphanage, a clinic, a school, a church, and eventually a hospital. He even built furniture for people's houses. Fr. Damien also helped people set up farms on the island, and he built a reservoir for a steady water supply. He dedicated his parish to St. Philomena.

Fr. Damien additionally became a one-man crusade on behalf of his unfortunate flock, demanding the Hawaiian government do more. His efforts paid off, and the government finally did become more active in bettering the conditions for the inhabitants of Molokai.

Like the late Saint Teresa of Calcutta, Fr. Damien's work and holiness were well known worldwide long before his death. Fortunately, this notoriety helped Fr. Damien in recruiting others for his work.

In 1883, Sister Marianne Cope (now known as Saint Marianne of Molokai), along with six other Sisters of St. Francis of Syracuse, New York, came to Molokai to help Fr. Damien. Soon, the Sisters had a hospital running.

In 1886, Joseph Dutton – more commonly known as "Brother Joseph" – arrived to help Fr. Damien. Joseph was such a blessing to the community, that on his deathbed, Fr. Damien told everyone that he could die in peace, knowing Brother Joseph was there to take his place.

Eventually Fr. Damien contacted leprosy. One who came to help him was James Sinnett, a nurse from Mercy Hospital in Chicago. It was James, called "Brother James" by Fr. Damien, who served as Fr. Damien's secretary in Damien's final days and nursed him to the very end.

Fr. Damien died on April 15, 1889, at the age of 49. Pope Benedict XVI canonized Damien on October 11, 2009.

When Hawaii became a State of the United States in 1959, it chose Damien as one of its two representatives in the Statuary Hall in the U.S. Capitol.

St. Damien of Molokai's feast day is May 10. He is a patron saint of people with Hansen's Disease.

11
Saint Francis Xavier, S.J.
April 7, 1506 - December 3, 1552
Missionary Extraordinaire

The co-founder of the Jesuit order, Francis Xavier, was one of the greatest missionaries of all time, a true "missionary's missionary."

Francis was born on April 7, 1506, in Spain to a wealthy family. When he was seventeen, he was sent to the University of Paris to study. There, he met another young Spanish nobleman by the name of Ignatius of Loyola.

Ignatius had to work hard on his friend Francis to persuade him to give his life to Christ. With persistence, Ignatius was successful. In 1534, Ignatius and Francis, along with five other young men, vowed to serve Christ in a special way. They called their group the Society of Jesus,

Jesuits, spiritual soldiers for Jesus Christ. All of the men were ordained as priests in Venice.

After practicing nursing with another priest, Simon Rodríguez, in Lisbon, Francis set sail for the East Indies as a Jesuit missionary. Though the king wanted to give him a servant and money, Francis refused them. He said, "… the best means to acquire true dignity is to wash one's own clothes and boil one's own pot, unbeholden to anyone."

The trip to the Indies took thirteen months because the ship had to winter in Africa. Despite severe seasickness, Francis preached every Sunday and nursed the slaves, convicts, and others aboard the ship. Finally, the ship reached its destination of Goa, a colony of Portugal off the southwestern coast of India, and Francis began living the life of a missionary. He ate only rice with water and slept on a mat on the floor. Soon he began to win souls. Sometimes he baptized so many people in a day that he could hardly lift his arms from fatigue.

Unfortunately, Francis was not gifted at languages. He discovered, as many do, that it is much more difficult to learn a new language as an adult than it is as a child. Nevertheless, he continually struggled to learn enough so that he could share the stories of Jesus, of God, and of heaven to the people. And he was successful.

Francis pursued his ministry to the Malay Peninsula and finally to Japan. Much of his missionary success was due not only to his love for the people, but also to the fact that he always tried to incorporate the cultural practices of the people into his missionary work. In India he found that the religious poverty of the missionaries had a great appeal. But in Japan, he discovered that holy poverty was held in contempt. So, he and his companions got dressed up in their very best clothes and went to the ruler of the people. Francis presented himself as a representative of the King of Portugal (which indeed he was) and gave the ruler letters from authorities in India and presents, namely, a music box, a clock, and some glasses. With this approach, Francis Xavier won his way into the good graces of the Japanese rulers who, in turn, permitted his work to flourish.

Fr. Francis Xavier, the missionary who went to many lands for Christ, had one great desire: to bring Christ to China. However, on December 3, 1552, at age 46, he died on an island just off the coast of China. Only four people came to his funeral.

Francis Xavier was declared a saint of the Catholic Church in 1622 along with St. Ignatius of Loyola, St. Teresa of Avila, and St. Philip Neri. His feast day is December 3.

St. Francis Xavier is a patron saint of foreign missionaries, epidemics, navigators, Japan, and many other places.

12
Saint Frances Xavier Cabrini, M.S.C.
July 15, 1850 – December 22, 1917
Immigrant Missionary

The first American citizen to be canonized was a missionary whose name, in Religious life, was Frances Xavier Cabrini.

Maria Francesca Cabrini was born on July 15, 1850 in Italy, the youngest of 13 children in a farm family. As a child, she would visit an uncle who lived by a swift-running canal. On these visits, she would make boats of paper, drop violets in them, and send the little paper boats off to India and China. She called the violets "missionaries."

As a teen, she wanted to join the order of Sisters who were her teachers, but they rejected her because she was too frail. Instead, she became the head of an orphanage. There, she gathered a small group of women to live as Religious, and in 1877, she took vows.

In November 1880, Sr. Frances Xavier and seven other women founded the Missionary Sisters of the Sacred Heart of Jesus (M.S.C.). They cared for orphans, opened a school, and did embroidery to earn money.

In 1887, Sr. Frances Xavier sought permission from Pope Leo XIII to take a band of her Sisters to be missionaries in China. Instead, he talked her into taking her band of Sisters to the United States to help the hordes of Italian immigrants who were moving there and living in poverty. So, she arrived with her Sisters in New York City on March 31, 1889, and became a naturalized American citizen in 1909.

For the next 35 years, in spite of staggering obstacles, Mother Cabrini, as she was known, founded 67 institutions all across the continental United States – schools, nursing centers, orphanages, and hospitals. This was what a woman who had been denied admission to a teaching order for being "too frail" was able to accomplish!

On December 22, 1917, at the age of 67, Mother Cabrini died of complications from malaria in Columbus Hospital in Chicago, one of the many hospitals she founded.

Pope Pius XII canonized Mother Cabrini on July 7, 1946. A crowd of 120,000 flooded Soldiers' Field in Chicago for a Mass of Thanksgiving at the time of her canonization. St. Frances Xavier Cabrini has the honor of being the first American citizen to be canonized. Later, St. Elizabeth Ann Seton would have the honor of being the first native-born American citizen to be canonized.

St. Frances Xavier Cabrini is a patron saint of immigrants. Hilariously, she is also informally recognized as a saintly intercessor to contact when trying to find a parking space. As one priest explained, "She lived in New York City. She understands traffic."

St. Francis Xavier Cabrini's feast day is November 13.

13
Blessed Francis Xavier Seelos, C.Ss.R.
January 11, 1819 - October 4, 1867
A Martyr to Charity

Francis Xavier Seelos was born in Füssen, Germany on January 11, 1819. He was the sixth child of a family that would eventually have 12 children. He was baptized on the same day at his parents' parish church of St. Mang.

Clues to Francis' eventual vocation to the priesthood were seen in childhood, when he would set up an altar at home and hold services for his little friends.

After completing his philosophy education at the University of Munich, Francis entered a diocesan seminary in 1842. One day, however, he read letters printed in a newspaper called *Sion*, published by Redemptorist missionaries, about how German-speaking immigrants in the United States lacked spiritual care. Therefore, he applied to, and was accepted by, the Redemptorist Order.

Francis departed for the United States on March 17, 1843, from the port of Le Havre on the ship *Saint Nicholas*, and arrived in New York City on April 20, 1843.

He spent his novitiate year in Baltimore, and on May 16, 1844, he took his first vows. On December 22, 1844, Francis was ordained a priest.

After serving at St. James Church in Baltimore for 6 months, the young missionary priest was sent to St. Philomena Church in Pittsburgh. This church was nicknamed "the factory church," for it was a makeshift church originally built as a factory.

Fr. Francis grew and flourished under the direction of his pastor, St. John Neumann, a Bohemian Redemptorist. Soon, stories began circulating about how exceedingly generous and kind Fr. Francis was to the poor and sick. Sometimes, for example, he would do private duty nursing for a sick child so the mother, who had an exhausting job outside the home, could have a break.

Fr. Francis performed all the usual pastoral duties – baptize infants, witness weddings, visit the sick, celebrate Reconciliation, counsel individuals and couples, and the myriad of other things done by parish priests. In addition, he also preached in English, German, and French.

People loved Fr. Francis' sermons because they were simple and highly entertaining despite his poor English. His sermons showed his very deep pastoral love for the people.

Though his parishioners loved him, from time to time he encountered anti-Catholic bigots who tried to harm him. Once, for example, he was brutally beaten, and at other times he was pelted by rocks, threatened at gunpoint, and nearly thrown overboard from a ferryboat while carrying the Blessed Sacrament with him.

In March of 1854, Fr. Francis became pastor of St. Alphonsus parish in Baltimore and was appointed director of students at the Redemptorist seminary.

Fr. Francis loved the sick so much, that it was said he would sleep in his clothes at night on a bench near the front door so he could go at a moment's notice if a sick parishioner needed him.

In March 1857, Fr. Francis was sent to Annapolis as pastor of a small parish named St. Mary and was appointed novice master for the Redemptorists. That assignment lasted only two months, and then his superiors sent him to a smaller church in Cumberland, Maryland – Saints Peter and Paul. He was also made director of a Redemptorist seminary.

In the seminary, Fr. Francis was wildly popular with the seminarians because he was very progressive for his time. Not only was he very approach-able, but he was also playful with the students. Once, for example, he asked if he could become a member of the Laughing Society that three students had formed.

Fr. Seelos's popularity with the students made other priests jealous of him. His peers' jealousy, however, did not make him change his joyful, Spirit-led, progressive style.

In 1865, Fr. Francis served in Detroit, and in September 1866, he was transferred to St. Mary's Church in the Irish section of New Orleans. During his time there, a yellow fever epidemic devastated the area. Fr. Francis nursed the sick and met their spiritual needs. As a result of his nursing, he contracted yellow fever and died on October 4, 1867. His nursing earned him the title of "martyr to charity."

Fr. Francis Xavier Seelos was buried at St. Mary's in New Orleans.

Pope St. John Paul II beatified Francis Xavier Seelos on April 9, 2000. Blessed Francis Xavier Seelos' feast day is October 5.

On January 11, 2013, the Seelos Center was dedicated at Research College of Nursing at Rockhurst University in Kansas City, Missouri. This facility has classrooms, meeting spaces, nursing simulation labs, lounges, and offices, all designed to assist nursing students to become great nurses.

42

14
Sister Henrietta of Hough, C.S.A.
July 19, 1902 - October 17, 1983
Missionary Hero of Inner-City Cleveland

Unlike many of the missionary heroes who traveled to distant countries as foreign missionaries, Marie Gorris did her mission work in her own "backyard," the inner-city area of Cleveland, Ohio called Hough. And she began this particular ministry when she was in her late 60s, showing that it's never too late to do the Lord's work.

Marie Gorris was born in Cleveland, Ohio on July 19, 1902. After graduating from St. Edward Parish High School, she attended Canton's Mercy Hospital School of Nursing and became a Registered Nurse in 1925.

Marie then entered the Sisters of Charity of St. Augustine (C.S.A.) from St. Philomena parish in East Cleveland and took her final vows in 1931. Her name in religious life was Henrietta.

From 1928 to 1962, Sr. Henrietta held a variety of nursing administration positions at Mercy Hospital. Then in 1962, Sr. Henrietta came to Cleveland to be the director of nursing at St. Vincent Charity Hospital. There she worked until 1965.

Hough is a poor inner-city area of Cleveland. It was there, from July 18 to July 23, 1966, that the infamous "Hough Riots" took place. It was in this poverty-stricken place that Sr. Henrietta chose to do her mission work.

Determined to help the people of Hough renew their community, Sr. Henrietta moved into the area. She taught people to be self-sufficient and encouraged them to care not only for themselves and their families, but also to help their neighbors in need.

Sr. Henrietta was the director of Our Lady of Fatima Mission Center from 1965 to 1983. This agency, and others like it, provided food, clothing, education, employment opportunities, health care, and housing for the area's residents. The center is still operating today in the Diocese of Cleveland.

For her missionary efforts, Sr. Henrietta received many awards, including the Catholic Interracial Council Award (1976), the National Coalition's Distinguished Community Service Award (1980), the American Jewish Committee's Micah Award (1983), and two honorary degrees.

Sr. Henrietta died on October 17, 1983 and is buried in Calvary Cemetery in Cleveland.

Msgr. Robert C. Wolff wrote a book about Sr. Henrietta's life called *Sr. Henrietta of Hough: She Reclaimed a Cleveland Slum*. Thanks to the CSA Archives for providing the photo of Sr. Henrietta.

15
Blessed James Miller, F.S.C.
September 12, 1944 - February 13, 1982
They Called Him "Brother Fix-It"

Like Sr. Henrietta of Hough, James Miller was another missionary hero of our times. James was born on September 12, 1944 in Stevens Point, Wisconsin in the United States, into a farm family.

In Pacelli High School, he came in contact with the De La Salle Christian Brothers for the first time, and greatly admired their work as teachers.

So, in September 1959, he entered the novitiate of the Order in Missouri. In Religious life, James took the name Leo William. However, after the Second Vatican Council, he went back to using his baptismal name.

His first assignment as a Brother was as a teacher at Cretin High School in St. Paul, Minnesota for three years. There, he taught English, Religion, and Spanish, supervised the school's maintenance, and coached football.

In 1969, after making his perpetual vows as a Christian Brother, Brother James was sent to Bluefields, an autonomous political region in Nicaragua. He taught there until he was re-assigned as director of a school in Puerto Cabezas, Nicaragua in 1974. Under his leadership, the school enrollment went from 300 to 800 students. He was more commonly known as Hermano Santiago, Spanish for Brother James.

Brother James also supervised the building of ten new rural schools.

In July of 1979, Brother James' religious superiors ordered him to leave Nicaragua because of personal danger from the civil war there. He returned to Minnesota and to teaching at Cretin High School. He also spent time in the Sangre de Cristo renewal program in New Mexico in 1980.

In January of 1981, Brother James was sent to Guatemala. There, he taught school in Huehuetenango and worked at the Indian Center where young indigenous Mayans from rural areas studied agriculture.

Brother James was known for his hard work, love of his religious vocation, and his simplicity. Though he was a very knowledgeable man, his simplicity captivated everyone who knew him.

Once, when he was working in Nicaragua with the very poor, someone asked him if he was afraid to be in a place with so much violence. Brother James replied, "Are you kidding? I never thought I could pray with such fervor when I go to bed."

In January of 1982, he was aware that the situation in Guatemala was dangerous. He wrote that although it was scary being in a violent environment, his commitment to the suffering poor of Central America was stronger than his fear.

Brother James, because he was so handy fixing things, was sometimes called "Brother Fix-It." His final action, in fact, was repairing a building.

The date was February 13, 1982. As Brother James climbed a ladder, three hooded men appeared and shot him several times. Brother James, at the age of 37, died instantly.

On December 7, 2019, Brother James Miller's beatification ceremony took place in Huehuetenango, Guatemala. Blessed James Miller's feast day is February 13.

One of the houses on the Holy Cross Campus in Reitoca, F.M., Honduras is dedicated to the memory of Blessed James Miller.

16
Ms. Jean Donovan
April 10, 1953 – December 2, 1980
She Marched to Her Own Drummer

Jean Donovan is another American missionary hero of our time. She was born on April 10, 1953 and grew up with her older brother Michael and their parents in Westport, Connecticut.

While attending Mary Washington College in Virginia (now known as the University of Mary Washington), Jean spent a year as an exchange student in Cork, Ireland. There, she made friends with Fr. Michael Crowley, a priest who had an extensive missionary background in Peru and other places. From this friendship, the missionary seed was planted and grew in Jean.

After receiving her college degree, Jean went to her father's hometown of Cleveland, Ohio, to obtain her master's degree from Case Western Reserve University.

Armed with solid academic credentials, and a larger-than-life personality, Jean soon found herself in a fabulous job at Arthur Andersen. Before long, she was living in a beautiful home on Cleveland's Gold Coast on the shores of Lake Erie. From outward appearances, she had everything a young woman on the rise could hope for.

Soon, though, Jean began volunteering with the Catholic Diocese of Cleveland's youth ministries. While doing volunteer work, Jean heard of the diocesan mission team that was serving in El Salvador. She felt God was calling her, and so she took action.

First, she took a four-month course for laypeople at Maryknoll, New York, although she did not become a Maryknoll Lay Missioner. After the course was finished, Jean found herself in El Salvador in July 1977 as part of the Diocese of Cleveland's mission team.

For the next three years, Jean served the Salvadoran people in every way she could — teaching religion, conducting classes, visiting the sick, and the like. But as time went on, El Salvador became more and more engulfed in a civil war, and Jean found her daily life changing drastically. Her daily chores became burying dead bodies, consoling mothers who had lost their sons, conducting services for men in the night after they had worked all day in the fields, and transporting priests and others who were just one step away from being murdered by the government.

Though she sometimes considered leaving the bloodbath around her, she reflected on the little children and the poor adults. Who would console them at night? Who would nurse the sick and injured of them? Who would bury them? Jean knew that she could never, in good conscience, abandon her beloved Salvadorans.

On the night of December 2, 1980, Jean and her friend, Ursuline Sister Dorothy Kazel from Cleveland, went to the airport in San Salvador to pick up two friends who were returning from a Maryknoll Sisters' conference in Nicaragua, Maryknoll Sisters Ita Ford and Maura Clarke. Little did they know that a government death squad was watching them and waiting for them.

After Jean and her three friends began their journey home, the death squad stopped them and drove them to a remote area. There, they raped and murdered all four women and buried them in a shallow grave.

The death of the four women martyrs made big news in the United States, and for the first time, many Americans began to realize the horror that was going on in this Central American nation.

A film called *Roses in December* is based on Jean's life, and author Ana Carrigan has written a very powerful and inspirational book about Jean called *Salvador Witness: The Life and Death of Jean Donovan*.

17
Blessed Joseph Gerard, O.M.I.
March 12, 1831 - May 29, 1914
A Spark in South Africa

Joseph Gerard was born on March 12, 1831 near Nancy, France and spent his childhood on the family farm. With the help of a parish priest, Joseph was able to enter the seminary to study for the priesthood. While still a seminarian, Joseph learned of a newly established missionary society – the Missionary Oblates of Mary Immaculate (O.M.I.). Awed by inspirational missionary tales of adventure, Joseph decided to join their congregation.

When Joseph was 22 years old, the founder of the Oblates, Saint Eugene de Mazenod, ordained him a deacon and gave him his first assignment as a missionary to Natal in South Africa. In May of 1853, Deacon Joseph set out for Africa, never to see France again.

On February 19, 1854, Joseph was ordained a priest in South Africa. His special ministry was to work with the Zulu people, but he also worked with the local white population.

He spent very hard years working in the area, journeying through the rough countryside, learning new languages, dealing with intense heat and cold, and often sleeping outdoors. He became very discouraged, for despite his love and care and hard work, his missionary efforts did not seem to bear much fruit. Only much later would Joseph learn that the seeds he had planted in the hearts of the Zulu people would flourish and bloom.

In 1862, Joseph went to Lesotho to work with the Basotho people, hoping for more success than he had had with the Zulu people. He labored as a missionary in Lesotho for the next 52 years.

It took him two years of hard work before he made his first convert among the Basotho people. However, within five years, a new congregation of Sisters began, and with them Joseph established a successful mission station in Roma. Today, this area has many novitiates and seminaries, high schools, an Oblate university, religious houses, and a hospital. The people attribute all of this to the seeds planted by Fr. Joseph.

But of all Fr. Joseph's work, his greatest love was for helping the sick. In fact, many reports say his nursing care – both biophysical and psychosocial – was heroic. Long distances, treacherous mountain trails, and terrible weather could not stop him from making sick calls either on foot on by horse.

Fr. Joseph spent his last years at the mission in Roma in Lesotho. He continued caring for the sick no matter where they were, even when arthritis bent him almost in half, his sight was nearly gone, and he had to be lifted onto his faithful horse Artaban. Up to a month before his death, at the age of 83, Fr. Joseph could be seen making nursing rounds to care for those in need.

Fr. Joseph died on May 29, 1914. Pope St. John Paul II beatified him on September 15, 1988. Blessed Joseph Gerard's feast day is May 29.

18
Saint Juan Diego
ca. 1474 - 1548
He Brought Roses

Missionaries are sent to bring a message, the good news of Jesus Christ. Because of the message of one man, millions of people converted to Catholic Christianity. This missionary's name was Cuauhtlatohuac, which means "Eagle Who Speaks" in Nahuatl, the Uto-Aztecan language that he spoke. Fortunately for us, the Spaniards gave him a new name – Juan Diego.

Juan Diego was born sometime around 1474 in what we know today as Mexico. When he grew up, he was a poor man who made his living as a weaver, laborer, and farmer. He was also a devout Catholic Christian who walked many miles each day to attend Mass.

On the morning of December 9, 1531, as he was walking to church near what today we call Mexico City, the largest city in North America, Juan Diego heard music coming from a hill called Tepeyac. Suddenly, he saw a cloud encircled by a rainbow and a woman dressed like an Aztec princess. She had the beautiful skin color of a *Mestiza*, and she spoke his Nahuatl language.

She told Juan Diego that she was the Virgin Mary and that she wanted a church built on that very site. She said she was the devoted Mother and wanted the people to know of her compassion, love, help and defense. She wanted to take away their sufferings and sorrows and pain.

So, Juan Diego, who was about 57 years old at the time, reported his vision to the bishop. The bishop, though, was skeptical, and told Juan to bring him proof. So, that's what Juan Diego did. He went back to the hill, where he found beautiful roses growing in the frozen soil. After picking an armload of roses, he took them to the bishop. When Juan opened his cloak, not only did the roses tumble out, but on the cloak appeared an amazing likeness of the Virgin Mary, the same likeness that had appeared in his vision. Today, we call her Our Lady of Guadalupe.

From Juan Diego's message, over 9,000,000 Mexicans become Catholic Christians. Today, Our Lady of Guadalupe, whose feast day is December 12, is the patron saint of all the Americas.

Juan Diego died in 1548. Pope St. John Paul II canonized Juan Diego in 2002. St. Juan Diego, whose feast day is December 9, is a patron saint of indigenous peoples.

19
Saint Ignatius of Loyola, S.J.
1491 – July 31, 1556
The Spark that Lit the Fire

The influence of Ignatius of Loyola on the missionary life of the Church continues around the world even today, although he died in 1556.

Ignatius was born in 1491 in Spain. As a young man, he had dreams of becoming a great knight. However, his dreams were dashed in 1521 when he was seriously wounded by a cannonball that injured both of his legs.

While recovering, Ignatius wanted to read romantic tales of chivalrous knights and their adventures. However, the place where he recovered had only books about the life of Christ and the lives of the saints. Reluctantly, he read them to pass the time. God, however, touched his heart through these books. He especially loved reading about St. Francis of Assisi. Soon, instead of desiring to be a military knight, he decided to be a knight for Christ.

As a result of the books, and a vision of Mary, Ignatius changed his life. Between 1524 and 1537, Ignatius studied all over Europe, and in 1537, he was ordained a priest. In 1539, he and some companions banded together and formed the Society of Jesus, popularly known as the Jesuits. Among the young men was Francis Xavier, one of the greatest Christian missionaries of all time.

Fr. Ignatius was elected as the first Superior General of the new religious order and spent his time in Rome establishing a college, orphanages, and other institutions. His greatest contribution to mission life, however, was the foundation of the Society of Jesus. Through the centuries, the Jesuit Order has sent missionary Brothers, priests, and laypersons to all corners of the planet. Much of the Jesuit mission work is by way of teaching in Jesuit colleges and universities. In 2020, for example, there were 28 Jesuit colleges and universities in the United States alone.

St. Ignatius of Loyola died on July 31, 1556, which is why his feast day is July 31. He is a patron saint of soldiers, retreatants, educators, and many dioceses and geographical locations throughout the Christian world.

20
Sister Ita Ford, M.M.
April 23, 1940 – December 2, 1980
A Maryknoll Martyr

Ita Ford was a missionary woman of our times who gave her all for the Lord. She was born in Brooklyn, New York City, on April 23, 1940. Her father was an insurance agent who retired early because of tuberculosis, and her mother was a public-school teacher. She had an older brother, William, and a younger sister, Irene.

Even in high school, Ita knew she wanted to become a Catholic Sister, specifically a Maryknoll missionary. This may have been due to the example of one of her relatives, Francis Xavier Ford, who was the very first seminarian of the Maryknoll Fathers and Brothers, and who became a missionary in China, where he became a bishop but died in a Communist prison camp in 1952.

After graduating from college, Ita was accepted by the Maryknoll Sisters when she was 21. Three years later, however, she had to leave because of poor health.

For seven years, Ita worked as an editor at a publishing company before re-joining Maryknoll in 1971. After serving in Bolivia in 1972, Sr. Ita moved to Chile where she worked with the poor. There, she met and became close friends with Maryknoll Sister Carla Piette.

In 1978-1979, Ita spent a "reflection year" in the United States before taking her final vows. When that year was over, she decided to answer the call of Archbishop Oscar Romero (who is now a saint), to help the Church in El Salvador. Her friend Carla also decided to go to El Salvador. Sr. Carla arrived in El Salvador on the day Oscar Romero was martyred, and Ita arrived on the day of Oscar Romero's funeral.

During the time Sisters Carla and Ita were in El Salvador, a civil war rocked the country. Carla and Ita spent their time burying the dead, transporting priests who were marked for death to safety, consoling the children, and doing whatever needed to be done. Then, on August 22, 1980, as Sisters Carla and Ita were returning home from transporting a former prisoner to his hometown, their truck was caught in a flash flood. Sr. Carla was able to push tiny Sr. Ita out the window to save her life, but Sr. Carla drowned.

Unfortunately, however, Sr. Ita herself would not have long to live. On the night of December 2, 1980, government death squads would kill Sr. Ita and three companions, Maryknoll Sr. Maura Clarke, Ursuline Sr. Dorothy Kazel, and lay missioner Jean Donovan. Both Sr. Dorothy and Jean were members of the Diocese of Cleveland mission team.

Books about Ita include *Here I am Lord: The Letters & Writings of Ita Ford* by Jeanne Evans; *The Same Fate as the Poor* by Judith Noone; and *Ita Ford: Missionary Martyr* by Phyllis Zagano.

21
Saint Madeleine-Sophie Barat, R.S.C.J.
December 12, 1779 – May 25, 1865
Missionary of the Sacred Heart

There are many ways of "being a missionary." Some leave home for foreign lands, while others spread the good news of Jesus Christ in their own lands. And some do mission work by founding institutes that send others throughout the world. The life of St. Madeleine-Sophie Barat, founder of the Society of the Sacred Heart, is an example of the latter.

The feast of the Sacred Heart of Jesus is a day when Christians remember that the love of Jesus Christ has no limits. God loves all people, and there is no way we can ever destroy this love.

Madeleine-Sophie Barat, usually simply called Sophie, was born in France on December 12, 1779. As a child, Sophie obtained a splendid education from her brother Louis, who would one day become an ordained priest.

Sophie grew up during the French Revolution, when being a Catholic Christian was a very dangerous thing. In fact, her brother Louis escaped from the guillotine only through the intervention of a friend.

In 1795, Sophie and Louis went to Paris. There, Louis practiced his ministry in secret. Sophie lived in a safe house with some other women, and she continued her studies with Louis – mathematics, Scripture studies, Fathers of the Church, and Latin. These courses augmented those Louis had already taught her, such as Spanish, history, natural sciences, Greek, and Italian.

Although Sophie wanted to become a Carmelite nun, the government had extinguished that Order in France. Undaunted, Sophie and three other women in the safe house started a new Order in 1800, the Society of the Sacred Heart. But because the government had banned devotion to the Sacred Heart of Jesus, the women at first called themselves simply "Women of Faith" or "Christian Instructors."

The primary purpose of this new Order was to serve God by serving as educators to the poor, especially poor girls. Soon the Order grew and flourished and sent missionaries all over the world. Today, the Sisters of the Sacred Heart are found in many nations of Africa, Europe, North America, and South America.

Some of St. Sophie's sayings show the kind of woman she was:

- More is gained by indulgence than by severity.
- Your example, even more than your words, will be an eloquent lesson to the world.
- Be humble, be simple, bring joy to others.

Sophie died on May 25, 1865 at the age of 85 and was canonized 1925 by Pope Pius XI. St. Sophie's feast day is May 25. She is a patron saint of schoolgirls.

22
Sister Marianne Cope, O.S.F.
January 23, 1838 - August 9, 1918
The Leper Sister

Maria Anna Barbara Koob, whose last name was later changed to Cope, was born on January 23, 1838 in Germany, but her family moved to Utica, New York when she was only a year old. In eighth grade, she went to work in a factory to help support her family, as her father had become an invalid. When her father became an American citizen, the whole family received American citizenship.

After her younger siblings were able to support themselves, and her father had died, Maria entered the Sisters of the Third Order Regular of St. Francis based in Syracuse, New York. Her name in religious life was

Marianne. She became a teacher and later a principal in newly established schools for German-speaking immigrants in the region.

By 1870, Sr. Marianne was elected to her Order's governing council. In that role, she helped to establish the first two Catholic hospitals in central New York State. These hospitals were instructed to serve everyone regardless of religion or race. From 1870 to 1877, Sr. Marianne led St. Joseph Hospital, the first public hospital in Syracuse, N.Y.

In 1883, when Sr. Marianne was the superior general of her Order and long before Hawaii was an American state, King Kalakaua of Hawaii sent a letter to her Order asking for help caring for persons with Hansen's disease, more commonly known as leprosy. More than fifty religious orders had already refused. Sr. Marianne, however, was delighted to help. She said, "I am hungry for the work and I wish with all my heart to be one of the chosen ones, whose privilege it will be to sacrifice themselves for the salvation of the souls of the poor Islanders ... I am not afraid of any disease; hence it would be my greatest delight even to minister to the abandoned 'lepers.'"

Sr. Marianne Cope, with six other Sisters from Syracuse, went to Hawaii, where they worked with lepers in hospitals on the islands of Oahu and Molokai.

In 1888, Sr. Marianne went to Kalaupapa on the island of Molokai. There, she cared for Fr. Damien (chapter 10), who was already an internationally known figure for his care for lepers and who was canonized in 2009. She also established a school for girls and women.

After Fr. Damien died, Sr. Marianne got the Brothers of the Sacred Heart to come to run Fr. Damien's school for boys. A layman named Joseph Dutton, usually called "Brother Joseph," was given charge of this house for boys. Joseph, a recovering alcoholic and veteran of the American Civil War, served faithfully for many years and is now on the path to sainthood.

Sr. Marianne Cope died on August 9, 1918 at the age of 80. She was canonized in 2012 by Pope Benedict XVI and is a patron saint of lepers, outcasts, persons with HIV/AIDS, and the State of Hawaii. Her feast day is January 23.

23
Mother Mary Joseph Rogers, M.M.
October 27, 1882 - October 9, 1955
She Used Her Gifts Wisely

Mary Joseph Rogers, called "Mollie" by her family, was the right person, in the right place, at the right time, for the right cause. She was born on October 27, 1882, in Roxbury, Massachusetts, one of eight children of Abraham Rogers and Josephine Plummer. The family had to practice their Catholic faith discreetly, for at the time, there was a general distrust of Irish Americans.

After attending public schools through the twelfth grade, Mollie went to Smith College in her home state, majoring in zoology. While at Smith, she was fascinated by a group of Protestant students who were planning to go to China for missionary work.

After graduating from Smith in 1905, the college invited her to work in the zoology department while working on a master's degree. So, Mary Joseph came back to Smith. While she was there, a faculty member who was interested in starting service clubs in the student body, asked her if she would start one. Mary decided to start a mission club for Catholic students, much like the one that the Protestants had. This endeavor led her to seek the help of the head of the Propagation of the Faith for Boston, Fr. James Anthony Walsh. Fr. James would later become a bishop and co-founder of the Catholic Foreign Mission Society of America, more commonly known as the Maryknoll Fathers and Brothers.

Mary Joseph began her work with Fr. James by assisting with the publication of his magazine, *The Field Afar*, along with some other similarly inclined young women.

In 1911, Fr. Walsh co-founded the Maryknoll Fathers and Brothers with Fr. Thomas Frederick Price of Wilmington, North Carolina.

In 1912, Fr. Walsh asked Mary Joseph Rogers to lead her little group of women to help him. Soon, the idea of a Maryknoll group for women was born. Because Mary Joseph did not know the procedures for founding a religious Order, she enlisted the help of the Dominican Sisters of Sinsinawa, Wisconsin. In February of 1920, her group of 35 women became an established congregation. Today, this group is known as the Maryknoll Sisters of St. Dominic or, simply, "the congregation" to distinguish it from the Maryknoll Fathers & Brothers, "the society." Mary Joseph became "Mother Mary Joseph" and served as the congregation's leader until she retired.

One of the beauties and strengths of Mother Mary Joseph's leadership was her understanding that the missionary life cannot possibly follow the highly regimented lifestyle found in cloistered groups. Because of that, the Maryknoll Sisters were required to develop their individual skills, and to remain in God's presence at all times while doing the various and unpredictable things that needed to be done in a mission from day to day. She said, "In our active religious life, we don't have time for sustained and long prayer. We must cultivate union with God at every possible moment."

Mother Mary Joseph died in New York Hospital on October 9, 1955. Before she died, she told the Maryknoll Sisters who brought her to the hospital to be sure the physicians got a break.

Today, the congregation that Mary Joseph founded has a missionary presence worldwide.

68

24
Saint Mary MacKillop, S.O.S.J.
January 15, 1842 - August 8, 1909
A Light from Down Under

The first Australian to be canonized was a missionary named Mary MacKillop. Mary was born in Melbourne on January 15, 1842, to a couple who had emigrated from Scotland to Australia, the eldest of eight children. Her father, Alexander, had studied for the priesthood, but just before ordination, at the age of 29, he left the seminary. One of Mary's brothers, Donald, became a Jesuit priest, and her sister Lexie became a Religious Sister.

As a young person, Mary worked at various jobs to help the family financially, for although her father was a very good man, he was never particularly successful in his occupations.

In 1860, Mary went to work as a governess at her aunt and uncle's home in South Australia. There, she met a priest who would greatly influence her vocational journey, Fr. Julian Tenison-Woods. From this contact, Mary began to teach poor children on the advice of this priest. Soon, Mary had more than 50 children in her care, and she decided God was calling her to be a Religious Sister.

In 1867, Mary founded a new Order, the Sisters of St. Joseph of the Sacred Heart. She was the first Sister and Mother Superior. They were more frequently simply called the Josephite Sisters or, because of their brown habit, the "Brown Joeys." In Religious life, she called herself Sr. Mary of the Cross.

The next few years were very difficult for Mary because of an incredible amount of drama: priest scandals, a bishop whose infirmities basically let his diocese become chaotic, clerical discord, clerical power struggles, and allegations of improper behavior. These years of Mary's life could easily be made into a dramatic television series. The situation became so bad, in fact, that Sr. Mary of the Cross was actually excommunicated from the Church for a short period of time! Historians believe the excommunication was because of anger over her reporting of sexual abuse by a priest.

Fortunately, however, God was looking out for the Josephite Sisters. By 1871, there were more than 130 members teaching in more than 40 schools in Australia. Sr. Mary's Order was unique at the time in that the Sisters did not have formal convents, and were under the authority of a Superior General, rather than a bishop.

In addition to teaching, the Josephite Sisters ran orphanages, cared for unwed mothers who had been rejected by their families, and worked with the indigenous Australians. The Sisters are proud to say they provided the social services that the Australian government could not provide at the time, and they provided these services equally to all: Catholics, Protestants, and those of no religion.

Sister Mary MacKillop died on August 8, 1909, and was canonized as the first Australian saint on October 17, 2010. Saint Mary MacKillop's feast day is August 8.

25
Sister Mary Mercy Hirschboeck, M.M.
March 10, 1903 - September 20, 1986
Mercy Was Her Name

Dr. Josephine Elizabeth Hirschboeck was the first physician to enter the Maryknoll Sisters Congregation, an order devoted to lives of service in other countries. She was born on March 10, 1903, in Milwaukee. After high school, Josephine entered Marquette University. While a student there, she was in a serious car accident. Josephine interpreted her survival as a sign that God was calling her to the Religious life. So, she applied to the Maryknoll Sisters. She was told to finish her medical education before applying. So, that is what she did.

After completing her internship, Josephine entered Maryknoll and received the name Sister Mary Mercy. Her first assignment, in 1931, was to Korea, where she served the people as a physician. She became very popular with the Koreans.

From 1940 to 1943, she worked in the Maryknoll Motherhouse in New York as infirmarian. Then in 1943 Sr. Mercy went with three other Sisters to Riberalta, Bolivia, where they began practicing medicine out of a one-room clinic. In time, the clinic became a hospital. When she left in 1950, the President of Bolivia said it was the best run hospital in the country.

Although civilians were not permitted to go to Korea in the early 1950s, Sr. Mercy received permission from General Douglas MacArthur to return there, taking along two other Maryknoll Sisters. In 1951, the Sisters found themselves treating thousands of refugees fleeing from North Korea. In 1952, Marquette University gave her an honorary Doctor of Science degree.

When she returned to the United States in 1955, Sr. Mercy became the administrator of Queen of the World Hospital in Kansas City, Missouri, the first fully-integrated general hospital in the city.

From 1958 to 1970, Sr. Mercy served as Vicaress General of the Maryknoll Sisters Congregation. When her time in administration was completed, Sr. Mercy served as a unit coordinator of the senior Sisters living at the Sisters' Center. Then, in 1973, Sr. Mercy found herself once again in active ministry, this time on the Lower East Side of New York City with other Sisters, living with the poor and providing help with their spiritual lives.

Sr. Mercy died on September 20, 1986, the feast of the Korean Martyrs, after giving 58 years of service to the Maryknoll Congregation and the world.

26
Sister Maura Clarke, M.M.
January 13, 1931 - December 2, 1980
Champion of the Underdog

A prominent missionary hero of Central America was an American named Maura Clarke. Mary Elizabeth Clarke was born on January 13, 1931, in the Bronx, New York City, and grew up in the Rockaway section of Queens.

In addition to learning about her Catholic faith, Mary also learned much about Irish history and the ways in which her family and their friends fought valiantly against oppression in Ireland. She came to understand that she came from people who believed in, and fought for, equality and dignity for all people. This love of the "underdogs" of society would be a recurrent theme in her life.

When she grew up, Mary became a Maryknoll Missionary Sister, known as Sister Maura John. After serving for a time in the Bronx, Maura was sent to Siuna, a remote town in Nicaragua, in 1959. Most of Sr. Maura's missionary life would be spent in Nicaragua.

Maura fell in love with the people of Nicaragua, and they fell in love with her. Maura loved teaching about Jesus and thrived on helping people. She was thrilled by the Second Vatican Council's call for Catholic Christians to return to their ancient roots. She was particularly inspired by Vatican II's call for the laity to be full members of the Church, and to engage in the social justice mission of Catholic Christianity. True to her own roots, Maura believed in empowerment of ordinary people.

As the years went on, Nicaragua became more and more brutal. Government forces became hostile toward the poor, killing tens of thousands of peasants. Eventually, however, the peasants successfully overthrew the brutal but final Somoza family dictator.

Following peace in Nicaragua, Maura felt called to El Salvador, which was on the brink of the same nightmare that Nicaragua had just experienced. Though her friends begged her not to go to El Salvador, she said, "We've won here [in Nicaragua]. They [the poor] haven't won in El Salvador."

In August of 1980, Maura went to El Salvador to serve the people, just five months after the Archbishop of San Salvador, Oscar Romero, was martyred. And just as her Irish ancestors had fought for justice, and just as Maura had fought for justice in Nicaragua, she was now ready for El Salvador.

After serving the people of El Salvador for only a few months, however, Maura was murdered by government forces on December 2, 1980. Killed with Maura were three other American martyrs: Maryknoll Sr. Ita Ford; Ursuline Sr. Dorothy Kazel of Cleveland; and Lay Missionary Jean Donovan from the Diocese of Cleveland's mission team in El Salvador.

For more information on Sr. Maura, Eileen Markey's book *A Radical Faith: The Assassination of Sr. Maura* is highly recommended, along with *Hearts on Fire: The Story of the Maryknoll Sisters* by Penny Lernoux, et.al.; *The Same Fate as the Poor* by Judith M. Noone; and *Witnesses of Hope: The Persecution of Christians in Latin America* by Martin Lange and Reinhold Iblacker..

27
Saint Maximilian Kolbe, O.F.M., Conv.
January 8, 1939 – August 14, 1942
The Father Who Gave His Life for a Dad

Twentieth-century missionary Maximillian Kolbe was born as Raymond Kolbe on January 8, 1939 in Poland, the second son of a weaver and a midwife.

In adulthood, Raymond joined the Conventual Franciscan Order, took the name Maximilian, and was ordained a priest. He eventually earned doctorates in both philosophy and theology.

His priesthood was an active one. Not only did he have his own publishing house, he also founded Franciscan houses in China and Japan, and started radio stations. In 1936, Fr. Kolbe had to return to Europe from Asia because of poor health.

Adolf Hitler's campaign of hate across Europe sentenced millions to concentration camps to be tortured and killed. Among the groups that Hitler targeted were gay men, Jews, Gypsies, left-leaning public leaders and politicians, and Catholic priests.

In May of 1942, the Nazis captured Maximilian Kolbe, who became known as "Number 1-6-6-7-0," and sent him to the concentration and extermination camp known as Auschwitz.

Often the guards would torture prisoners and kill them for their own amusement. Maximilian accepted his fate as God's mysterious choice for him. And though it was illegal to do so, Maximilian ministered to everyone he could reach, including his fellow Franciscan friars. He urged prisoners to trust in God, despite their subhuman physical circumstances, and to believe that in the end, God's justice would prevail.

Maximilian would try to be at the beginning of the food line so that he could take from the watery top layer of the soup, leaving the richer portions below for other prisoners. Often, he gave away his scraps of food for others to eat.

At the end of July 1942, someone escaped from Maximilian's cellblock. As punishment, every man was forced to stand at attention for hours in the heat. In the evening, ten men were chosen arbitrarily by the guards for slow execution in starvation bunker #11. As the men began to remove their clothing, Fr. Maximilian stepped out of line and said to the guards, "I am old and useless. My life isn't worth much now." He asked that he be one of the ten men to be killed so that a young man who had a wife and two children could live. The guards agreed, and they let the young father, a Polish army sergeant named Franciszek Gajowniczek, be spared the starvation experience. Fr. Maximilian took his place.

Fr. Maximilian, with the other nine men, was stripped naked and put into a squalid death hole. The iron doors were closed, and the men were left to starve to death without food or water. Fr. Maximilian comforted his fellow sufferers, and for the first time in Auschwitz, the sound of hymns came from the bunker's air holes.

After two weeks, only four of the men were still alive, and Fr. Maximilian Kolbe was the only one still conscious. Because the Nazis needed the bunker to kill other men, they killed Fr. Maximilian by injecting phenol into his bloodstream. The date was August 14. The next day, his body was thrown into an oven, and his ashes were joined with those of countless others who had been killed at Auschwitz.

Maximillian was canonized in 1982. One of the people attending this event was the man whose life Maximillian had saved, Franciszek Gajowniczek.

St. Maximillian's feast day is August 14. He is a patron saint of amateur radio operators, drug addicts, political prisoners, families, and journalists.

82

28
Saint Noel Chabanel, S.J.
February 2, 1613 - December 8, 1649
The Missionary Who Didn't Like Mission Life

As a finicky eater myself, I can identify with the 17th century missionary St. Noel Chabanel.

Noel was born on February 2, 1613, in Saugues, France. When he was 17 years old, he entered the Society of Jesus. As a young Jesuit, Noel taught at several Jesuit colleges. Before long, he had gained a reputation not only for his knowledge, but also for his virtue.

In 1641, Noel was ordained a priest. In one of the journals of the day, Fr. Noel's superiors said of him, "Serious by nature – energetic – great stability – better than average intelligence."

At this time, many Jesuits were becoming missionaries in the French colony of Canada, which they called "New France." After he begged to be allowed to be a missionary in the New World, Noel's superiors finally gave him permission. To his credit, before leaving for Canada in 1643, Fr. Noel studied the native Algonquin language of the region he would serve, though he made little progress.

Once he arrived at his mission, he discovered that he could not master the language, hated the food, was repulsed by the lifestyles of the Indians, and came to experience spiritual dryness. However, with a strong faith, Fr. Noel made a vow before Jesus in the Blessed Sacrament that he would forever remain with the people he had come to serve unless his superiors ordered him elsewhere.

Fr. Noel did the best he could, assisting the other Jesuit priests in the area, much as a "gofer" helps a construction crew, by running errands, handing tools to the workers, and doing many other little things that don't require construction skills. Though this must have been quite humbling for a person known for his fine mind, Fr. Noel continued serving as well as possible, until a renegade Huron killed him at the age of 36.

Pope Pius XI canonized Fr. Noel on June 29, 1930. Saint Noel's feast day, along with seven other Jesuit Canadian missionary martyrs, is October 19.

29
Saint Paulina of the Agonizing Heart of Jesus, C.I.I.C.
December 16, 1865 - July 9, 1942
First Saint of Brazil

St. Paulina was born Amabile Lucia Visintainer on December 16, 1865 in Italy to a poor Catholic family. When she was almost ten years old, Amabile's family moved to Brazil with a number of other people from their village.

After she received her First Holy Communion at the age of twelve, Amabile devoted much of her time in her parish serving as a catechist, visiting the sick, and cleaning the chapel. These things she did in addition to working hard in the fields to help her poor parents.

When she was almost 25 years old, Jesuit missionaries in the area encouraged Amabile to consider Religious life. With this encouragement, Amabile and a friend left home to live in a small cottage. There, they began a new life dedicated to helping the sick and the poor, beginning by caring for a woman who had cancer.

Their modest beginning turned into a new Congregation of Religious Sisters called the Little Sisters of the Immaculate Conception. In 1895, Amabile received the approval of the Church for her new Congregation and took her vows. She took the name Paulina of the Agonizing Heart of Jesus.

In 1903, Sr. Paulina moved to São Paolo when her Jesuit spiritual director moved there. Her Congregation flourished and many houses of the Order were established. As the Founder of the Order, Sr. Paulina was the superior until 1909. At that time, however, a problem of some kind developed between the local archbishop and the Congregation. As a result, Sister Paulina was ordered to step down from being Superior of the Order she had founded and to become a simple Sister. Though this must have been very hard for her, Sr. Paulina did so with obedience and great humility. From 1909 until her death in 1942, Sr. Paulina served by caring for poor elderly people. By that time, her Congregation had 45 houses throughout Brazil, and by 1980, it had 105 houses with over 600 members.

In 1938, Sr. Paulina's health began to fade from the diabetes that she had suffered for most of her life. In two operations, she lost a finger and then her entire right arm. She lived the last months of her life totally blind. On July 9, 1942, she died saying, "God's will be done."

Paulina was canonized on May 19, 2002. St. Paulina's feast day is July 9. She is one of the patron saints of diabetics.

30
Saint Rose Philippine Duchesne, R.S.C.J.
August 29, 1769 - November 18, 1852
Woman-Who-Prays-Always

Rose Philippine Duchesne was born in Grenoble, France on August 29, 1769. From her father, she learned political skills, and from her mother, she learned a love for the poor.

When she was 19 years old, Rose joined a convent without telling her parents. Though her parents were opposed to her choice, she remained in the convent. Her strong will was one of the characteristics of her personality that stayed with her throughout her life.

When her convent was shut down by the French government following the French Revolution, she began privately taking care of the sick and poor. She opened a school for street children and risked her life helping priests in the underground.

After the Reign of Terror, French anti-Christian revolutionary sentiment became less prominent under Napoleon, and Rose joined Madeleine Sophie Barat, later named a Saint, in the Society of the Sacred Heart.

Sr. Rose soon became a leader in her community, and after hearing tales of missionary work in Louisiana, she developed a missionary spirit. Her great desire was to go to the United States and work with the Native Americans that she had heard so much about.

When she was 49 years old, Rose and four other nuns were sent to New Orleans and then to St. Louis, Missouri. She was greatly disappointed when the bishop there sent her to work not with Indians, but to a free school for girls in St. Charles, Missouri, the first such school west of the Mississippi River.

At age 72, however, Mother Rose finally saw her dream of working with indigenous people come true. Though she was retired and in poor health, she went to work among the Potawatomi tribe. However, she was not able to learn their language, so she decided to be the prayer warrior, while others taught the people. She soon became known as "Woman-Who-Prays-Always" because of her profound prayer life. Legend has it that Native American children would sneak up behind her while she was praying and sprinkle bits of paper on her habit. When they returned several hours later, they found the papers just where they had put them.

Mother Rose died on November 18, 1852, at the age of 83 and was canonized July 3, 1988. St. Rose Duchesne's feast day is November 18.

31

Blessed Stanley Rother
March 27, 1935 - July 28, 1981
The Shepherd Who Didn't Run

Fr. Stanley Rother was born on March 27, 1935, in Okarche, Oklahoma and attended the local church and school of Holy Trinity.

In high school, he decided to study for the priesthood. After spending time at Assumption Seminary in San Antonio, Texas, Stanley finished his priesthood studies at Mount St. Mary Seminary at Emmitsburg, Maryland and was ordained on May 23, 1963 for the Archdiocese of Oklahoma City.

For the first five years of his priesthood, he served as a parochial vicar in various parishes in Oklahoma. Then, in 1968, he requested and

"

received permission to join the archdiocese's mission team in Santiago Atitlán, Sololá, Guatemala.

In this area, Fr. Stanley worked with the Tz'utujil tribe, descendants of the Mayans. Even though he had had trouble with Latin in the seminary, he managed to learn Spanish and the Tz'utujil language. In fact, in time, he was able to translate the New Testament into Tz'utujil and preach in the language.

Because of his farming background in Oklahoma, Fr. Stanley was able to help the farmers, who lived in extreme poverty, with planting, harvesting, and even building an irrigation system. In addition to the usual ministerial duties of a parish priest, he assisted the people when they needed healthcare attention and even founded a small hospital and supported a radio station.

During the entire time he was in Guatemala, a civil war was underway. Fr. Stanley's name was on the "death list" of the military government. He and another priest went back to Oklahoma briefly, but Fr. Stanley insisted on returning to his beloved Guatemalan parishioners, saying, "The shepherd cannot run at the first sign of danger."

On July 28, 1981, around 1 a.m., three men entered the rectory and executed him. Fr. Stanley was one of ten Catholic priests murdered by the government in Guatemala that year.

Fr. Stanley's body was moved for burial in Holy Trinity Cemetery in Okarche, Oklahoma, but his heart was buried under the altar of the church in Guatemala, according to the custom of the Tz'utujil people.

On September 23, 2017, Fr. Stanley was beatified. Blessed Stanley Rother's feast day is July 28. One of the guest houses on the Holy Cross campus in Reitoca, F.M., Honduras is dedicated to Blessed Stanley.

To learn more about Blessed Stanley's life, the excellent book by Maria Ruiz Scaperlanda, *The Shepherd Who Didn't Run: Father Stanley Rother: Martyr from Oklahoma*, is highly recommended.

32
Saint Teresa of Calcutta, M.C.
August 26, 1910 - September 5, 1997
Missionary to the Poorest of the Poor

Of all the saints in modern history, none is more popular and well-known as Mother Teresa of Calcutta, another missionary hero of our time.

Agnes Gonxha Bojaxhiu was born on August 26, 1910 in Skopje, North Macedonia to Albanian parents. Though her father's construction business allowed the family to live comfortably, the father died when Agnes was eight years old, leaving the family in poverty.

By the age of 18, Agnes had a long-time desire to be a missionary, so she left home and joined the Sisters of Loreto in Ireland. She received the name Mary Teresa after St. Therese of Lisieux. In 1929, Sr. Teresa left Ireland for Calcutta, and made her first vows in May of 1931. In India, she was assigned to a school for wealthy girls operated by the Loreto Sisters, where she taught history and geography.

Sr. Teresa made her final profession of vows in 1937, becoming a "spouse of Jesus." She continued teaching at the school, St. Mary's, and became the school's principal in 1944. In religious life, Teresa was noted for her charity, hard work, joy, and organizational skills. As her life unfolded, these skills would produce amazing blessings for the world.

Though Mother Teresa was happy in her life as a Loreto Sister, one day she experienced what she described as a "call within a call." On September 10, 1946, while she was traveling from Calcutta to Darjeeling for her annual retreat, Sr. Teresa experienced a strong, overpowering call from Jesus to serve the poorest of the poor.

So, back in Calcutta, her habit became the white sari and sandals of ordinary Indian women, and soon she made friends with neighbors to learn of their needs. She paid special attention to the poor and the sick. Soon, some of her former students joined her, and more comfortable people began donating clothing, food, supplies, and the use of a building.

On October 7, 1950, Mother's Teresa's group of Sisters became the Congregation of the Missionaries of Charity (M.C.). The Sisters cared for the "unwanted, the unloved, the uncared-for." The caste or religion of an individual in need did not matter: the Sisters treated every person with dignity and respect.

In time, Mother Teresa founded active and contemplative branches of her Order for Brothers, priests, and lay persons throughout the world. By 1997, Mother Teresa's Order had nearly 4,000 Sisters serving in 610 foundations in 123 nations. In 1979, Mother Teresa received the Nobel Peace Prize for her missionary work for the poor of the world.

Of all the many quotes attributed to St. Teresa of Calcutta, here are three that give the measure of the woman:

- Peace begins with a smile.
- Kind words can be short and easy to speak, but their echoes are truly endless.
- Spread love everywhere you go. Let no one ever come to you without leaving happier.

Mother Teresa died on September 5, 1997, and she was given a state funeral by India. About 15,000 people attended the funeral Mass, held in a stadium.

Pope Francis canonized Teresa on September 2, 2016. Saint Teresa of Calcutta's feast day is September 5.

33
Saint Therese of the Child Jesus, O.C.D.
January 2, 1873 - September 30, 1897
The Little Flower

One of the most famous and popular saints of our time is St. Therese Martin, known in Religious life as Sr. Therese of the Child Jesus and the Holy Face. She is commonly known as Therese of Lisieux or "The Little Flower." Because of frail health, Therese was never herself a missionary, but she is a patron saint of missionaries everywhere because of her devotion to them.

Therese was born in France on January 2, 1873, into a very devout family. In fact, both of her parents, Louis and Zélie, were canonized by Pope Francis in 2015, and her sister Léonie, a Visitation Sister, has been named a Servant of God by the Church. Therese was a Discalced Carmelite nun, as were three of her sisters.

Therese entered the Carmel in Lisieux at the age of 15. Sr. Therese wanted to do something very special for Jesus. For example, she wanted to be a priest! She wanted to be a missionary in Vietnam, but she couldn't because her health was not strong enough for the missionary life. And she wanted to be a martyr, but that was not likely to happen to a nun cloistered in a French Carmel in the late 19th century.

So, after much prayer and reflection, Therese decided she would simply be a great lover of Jesus. To do that, she would do every task the best way she could, all for the honor and glory of God. So, for example, if she was washing dishes, she did the best she could for the glory of the Lord. She called this the "little way" of spirituality. And because this "little way" can be adopted by any human being regardless of their station in life, it became quite popular.

Therese felt that by living the little way, she could be a "little flower" in God's garden, not a big rose or lily like a great saint, but rather a simple violet or daisy giving glory to God.

Therese also felt very close to priests, especially missionary priests. So, she devoted much of her prayer life to missions and missionary priests. And before her untimely death, she said she planned on spending her time in heaven serving all the people on earth, sending forth a shower of roses to those in need.

Therese died of tuberculosis on September 30, 1897 at the age of 24. After her death, one of her sisters from the same Carmel as Therese, had Therese's autobiography published. This book, called *The Story of a Soul*, is one of the most profound works in Catholic Christianity. In fact, as a result of it, Therese was declared a Doctor (teacher) of the Church.

Pope Pius XI canonized Therese on May 17, 1925. St. Therese, the Little Flower, is a patron saint of missionaries, florists, persons with AIDS, and the sick. St. Therese's feast day is October 1.

34
Servant of God Thomas Frederick Price, M.M.
August 19, 1860 - September 12, 1919
The Tarheel Apostle

I'm especially delighted to share the story of Thomas Frederick Price because he was from the same neighborhood of Wilmington, North Carolina where I was pastor of the Basilica Shrine of St. Mary parish from 2006 to 2018.

Thomas, who was called "Freddy" as a child, was born on August 19, 1860, the eighth of ten children. His father, a newspaper publisher and former Episcopalian, and his mother, a former Methodist, raised their children in a strong Catholic home. In fact, when Freddy was a boy, he used to be an altar server at Wilmington's old St. Thomas the Apostle Church, the forerunner of St. Mary, for Bishop James Gibbons, the first vicar-apostolic of North Carolina. He accompanied Bishop Gibbons, later Cardinal Gibbons of Baltimore, on his rounds throughout the vicariate.

In 1876, Freddy left home to begin studying to become a Catholic priest at St. Charles Seminary in Catonsville, Maryland. In those days, a journey from coastal North Carolina to Maryland was generally undertaken by sea. The first ship he was on was shipwrecked, but in 1877 he finally made it, and lived there until his graduation in 1881. That September, he entered St. Mary's Seminary in Baltimore and graduated in 1886. On June 20, Bishop Northrup ordained Freddy at St. Thomas in Wilmington.

From the time he was ordained a priest, Fr. Price demonstrated an exemplary strong work ethic, dedication, and clear vision. For him, North Carolina was his mission land. So, after serving as a pastor for a few years, he was given permission to begin a begin a statewide evangelization program. He published a magazine called *Truth* and founded the Nazareth Orphanage in Raleigh, North Carolina, in 1889.

In the summer months, Fr. Price welcomed seminarians to join him in the home missions, and in 1902, he founded a missionary training house for seminarians. This training house was to prepare seminarians to one day to work as "home missionaries," that is, as missionaries working in the United States, particularly in North Carolina. In time, Fr. Price would be given the nickname, "The Tarheel Apostle," for North Carolina is often called the "Tarheel State."

As time went on, however, Fr. Price's missionary vision grew to include the whole world, and at the Eucharistic Congress held in Montreal in 1910, he met Fr. James Anthony Walsh (later a bishop). The two men held similar visions, and their partnership led to the founding of the Catholic Foreign Mission Society of America, more commonly called the Maryknoll Fathers and Brothers. Eventually, three other groups would have the Maryknoll name: the Maryknoll Sisters; the Maryknoll Lay Missioners; and the Maryknoll Affiliates. Maryknoll, New York, site of the society's headquarters, is near Ossining.

When the Society (as the Fathers and Brothers are often called) began, Fr. Walsh was selected to be the administrator, while in 1918 Fr. Price got his wish of being one of the first group of three Maryknollers to go to the foreign missions. He went to China. Because Fr. Price was 58 years old, he had trouble learning the language. In addition, he suffered some physical ailments. He died of a burst appendix on September 12, 1919 in Hong Kong. He is buried at Maryknoll, New York.

Thomas Frederick Price is called a Servant of God by the Church, along with James Anthony Walsh. In downtown Wilmington, N.C. there are two historical markers, one honoring Fr. Price and the other honoring Cardinal Gibbons.

Today, the Order founded by these two men has missionaries all over the globe.

35
Servant of God Vincent Robert Capodanno, M.M.
February 13, 1929 – September 4, 1967
The Grunt Padre

Vincent Robert Capodanno was born on February 13, 1929 in Staten Island, New York City. In 1957, he became a Maryknoll missionary priest.

After serving in the mountains of Taiwan and in Hong Kong, Fr. Vince received permission to become a military chaplain. After completing chaplaincy school, he was commissioned as a lieutenant in the Navy Chaplain Corps and sent to serve with the U.S. Marines in Vietnam in 1966.

Fr. Vince had a fierce loyalty to the Marines he served, and he always wanted to be with them whenever and wherever they needed him. In time, he earned the nickname "The Grunt Padre."

As Americans were celebrating Labor Day in the United States on September 4, 1967, Fr. Vince went with a band of Marines who were being overwhelmed by North Vietnamese soldiers. Fr. Vince was badly wounded, but he refused to leave. Instead, he anointed and cared for the wounded and dying until he, too, was killed in the gunfire. He was 38 years old.

In December of 1968, the Secretary of the Navy notified Fr. Vincent's family that he was being given the Medal of Honor. The citation reads, in part:

> In response to reports that the 2nd Platoon of M Company was in danger of being overrun by a massed enemy assaulting force, Lt. Capodanno left the relative safety of the company command post and ran through an open area raked with fire, directly to the beleaguered platoon. Disregarding the intense enemy small-arms, automatic-weapons, and mortar fire, he moved about the battlefield administering last rites to the dying and giving medical aid to the wounded. When an exploding mortar round inflicted painful multiple wounds to his arms and legs, and severed a portion of his right hand, he steadfastly refused all medical aid. Instead, he directed the corpsmen to help their wounded comrades and, with calm vigor, continued to move about the battlefield as he provided encouragement by voice and example to the valiant Marines. Upon encountering a wounded corpsman in the direct line of fire ... he was struck down by a burst of machine gun fire. By his heroic conduct on the battlefield, and his inspiring example, Lt. Capodanno upheld the finest traditions of the U.S. Naval Service. He gallantly gave his life in the cause of freedom.

Fr. Capodanno has been honored by having a ship named after him, as well as chapels and monuments in Iraq, Vietnam, Italy, Japan, Taiwan, and several American states. The biggest honor, though, was being named "Servant of God" on May 19, 2006. That means that Fr. Capodanno is now on the way to becoming a Saint of the Catholic Church. One can read more about this Maryknoll missionary priest in the excellent book by Fr. Daniel Mode called *The Grunt Padre*.

Selected Bibliography

The purpose of this Selected Bibliography is to provide a starting place for persons interested in learning more about these Catholic Christian missionary heroes. It is not meant to be a comprehensive bibliography.

1 - Ms. Annalena Tonelli

- Comboni Missionaries' Team. "Witnesses: Annalena Tonelli, Mother Teresa of Somalia," 5 June 2020.
- Contributors to Wikipedia. "Annalena Tonelli." *Wikipedia: The Free Encyclopedia*, 24 June 2022
- Jones, Rachel Pieh. *Stronger than death: How Annalena Tonelli defied terror and tuberculosis in the Horn of Africa.* Plough Publishing House, 2019.
- UNICEF. "Annalena Tonelli: An inspired ally in the humanitarian effort in Somalia," 9 October 2003.

2 - Saint Anthony of Padua, O.F.M.

- Contributors to Wikipedia. "Anthony of Padua." *Wikipedia: The Free Encyclopedia*, 23 June 2022.
- St. Anthony Shrine. "Who is St. Anthony of Padua?" *stanthony.org*, no date.
- "St. Anthony of Padua." *Butler's Lives of the Saints: New Full Edition: June*, Revised by Kathleen Jones. Burns & Oates/The Liturgical Press, 1997, pp. 101-103.

3 - Saint Augustine of Canterbury, O.S.B.

- Contributors to Wikipedia. "Augustine of Canterbury." *Wikipedia: The Free Encyclopedia*, 25 March 2022.
- Newman, John Henry. *The life of St. Augustine of Canterbury, apostle of the English: With some account of the Early British Church.* Forgotten Books, 2018.
- "St. Augustine of Canterbury." *Butler's Lives of the Saints: New Full Edition: May,* Revised by David Hugh Farmer. Burns & Oates/The Liturgical Press, 1996, pp. 150-154.
- Toovey, James. *Lives of the English saints: St. Augustine of Canterbury, pp. 1-144.* Hardpress, 2018.

4 - Father Bill Woods, M.M.

- Brett, Donna Whitson. *The Bill Woods story: Maryknoll missionary in Guatemala.* Maryknoll Fathers & Brothers. No date.
- LaBuda, M.M., Fr. David. (Film) - "Fr. Bill Woods, M.M. – 1931-1976 – Martyr of the Ixcán, 2019."
- "Father William H. Woods, M.M." Maryknoll Mission Archives, 2021.
- "Father Bill Woods, M.M.: Missionary pilot, Texas cowboy for Jesus and martyr of the Ixcan – September 14, 1931 – November 20, 1976." Airlife Flyers Aviation Corp., 2012.
- Ofori, Michael. "Father Bill Woods." *Prezi,* October 28, 2015.

5 - Saint Boniface, O.S.B.

- Contributors to Wikipedia. "Saint Boniface," *Wikipedia: The Free Encyclopedia,* 4 June 2022.
- "St. Boniface." *Butler's Lives of the Saints: New Full Edition: June,* Revised by Kathleen Jones. Burns & Oates/The Liturgical Press, 1997, pp. 41-44.
- Saint Boniface and Ephraim Emerton, *The letters of St. Boniface.* Literary Licensing, LLC, 2013.
- Williamson, James M. *The life and times of St. Boniface.* Wentworth Press, 2019.

6 - Saint Camillus de Lellis, M.I.

- Cruz, Joan Carroll. "Saint Camillus de Lellis (1550-1614)," *Saints for the sick*, pp. 58-59. TAN Books, 2010.
- Contributors to Wikipedia. "Camillus de Lellis." *Wikipedia: The Free Encyclopedia*, 26 February 2022.
- Donnelly, John Patrick S.J. "Camillus de Lellis (1550 – 1614), Patron saint of hospitals." *The Linacre Quarterly*, 2011.
- Kus, Fr. Robert J. "St. Camillus de Lellis, M.I." *Saintly men of nursing: 100 amazing stories*, pp. 45-46. Red Lantern Press, 2017.
- McKeown, Jonah. "St. Camillus de Lellis: Patron saint of hospitals, nurses, and the sick." *Catholic News Agency*, April 18, 2020.
- "St Camillus de Lellis: Demonstrating Christ's love to the sick." The Basilica of the National Shrine of the Immaculate Conception, July 16, 2020.
- "St. Camillus de Lellis." *Butler's Lives of the Saints: New Full Edition: July*, Revised by Peter Doyle. Burns & Oates/The Liturgical press, 1999, pp. 100-102.

7 - Sister Carla Piette, M.M.

- Brett, Donna Whitson and Edward T. Brett. "Pope Francis' new pathway to sainthood clears the way for a woman religious." *U.S. Catholic*, December 1, 2020.
- Maggiore, Jacqueline Hansen. *Vessel of clay: The inspirational journal of Sister Carla*. University of Scranton Press, 2010.
- Noone, Judith M., M.M. *The same fate as the poor*. Orbis Books, 1984, 1995.
- "Sister Carol Piette, M.M." Maryknoll Mission Archives, 2021.

8. - Blessed Carlo Acutis

- Conquer, Will. *A millennial in paradise: Carlo Acutis*. Sofia Institute Press, 2019.
- Contributors to Wikipedia. "Carlo Acutis." *Wikipedia: The Free Encyclopedia*, 14 May 2022.
- Gori, Nicola. *Carlo Acutis: The first millennial saint*. Our Sunday Visitor, 2021.
- Kunnappally, Ephrem. *Highway to heaven: A spiritual journey through the life of Blessed Carlo Acutis*. Pavanatma Publications, 2022.
- Swain, Colleen and Matt Swaim. *Dare to be more: The witness of Blessed Carlo Acutis*. Liguori Publications, 2021.

9 - Servant of God Casimir Cypher, O.F.M., Conv.

- Brett, Donna Whitson and Edward T. Brett. "Father Casimir Cypher, a model for missionaries today," *U.S. Catholic*, January 14, 2022.
- Romb, Anselm W. *Man of peace: Casimir Michael Cypher, OFM Conv: His meaning in life was found in death.* 1985. [Out of print.]
- "The cause for canonization for Father Casimir Cypher, OFM Conv (+1975)." http://www.marytown.com, no date.

10 - Saint Damien of Molokai, SS. CC.

- "Bd. Damien De Veuster." *Butler's Lives of the Saints: New Full Edition: April,* Revised by Peter Doyle. Burns & Oates/The Liturgical press, 1999, pp. 104-108.
- Bunson, Matthew and Margaret. *Saint Damien of Molokai: Apostle of the exiled.* Our Sunday Visitor Publications, 2009.
- Contributors to Wikipedia. "Father Damien." *Wikipedia: The Free Encyclopedia,* 14 May 2022.
- Richards, FSP Virginia Helen. *Saint Damien of Molokai: Hero of Hawaii.* Pauline Books, 2009.
- Kus, Fr. Robert J. "St. Damien of Molokai, SS.CC.," *Saintly Men of Nursing: 100 Amazing Stories,* Red Lantern Press, 2017, pp. 52-55.

11 - Saint Francis Xavier, S.J.

- Contributors to Wikipedia. "Francis Xavier." *Wikipedia: The Free Encyclopedia,* 24 June 2022
- Kus, Fr. Robert J. "St. Francis Xavier, S.J.", *Saintly Men of Nursing: 100 Amazing Stories,* Red Lantern Press, 2017, pp. 73-75.
- "St. Francis Xavier." *Butler's Lives of the Saints: New Full Edition: December,* Revised by Kathleen Jones. Burns & Oates/The Liturgical press, 1999, pp. 25-30.
- "St. Francis Xavier." Saint of the Day for December 3.
- "St. Francis Xavier." Catholic Online/Saints and Angels, December 3.

12 - Saint Frances Xavier Cabrini, M.S.C.

- Ball, Ann. "Saint Frances Xavier Cabrini, M.S.C. (1850-1917)." *Modern saints: their lives and faces, Book One.* TAN Books: 1983.
- Contributors to Wikipedia. "Frances Xavier Cabrini." *Wikipedia: The Free Encyclopedia*, 21 June 2022.
- Galilea, Segundo. *In Weakness, strength: The life and missionary activity of Saint Frances Xavier Cabrini*, Claretian, 2004.
- Lawn, John & Keys, Frances Parkinson. *Mother Cabrini: Missionary to the World (Vision Books).* Ignatius Press, 1997.
- Missionary Sisters of the Sacred Heart. *An American saint of our time: Mother Frances Xavier Cabrini.* Kessinger Legacy Reprints, 2010.
- "St. Frances Xavier Cabrini." *Butler's Lives of the Saints: New Full Edition: December*, Revised by Kathleen Jones. Burns & Oates/The Liturgical press, 1999, pp. 168-171.

13 - Blessed Francis Xavier Seelos, C.Ss.R.

- Ball, Ann. "Francis X. Seelos, C.Ss.R. (1819-1867). *Modern saints: their lives and faces*, pp. 51-56. TAN Books: 1983.
- Contributors to Wikipedia. "Francis Xavier Seelos." *Wikipedia: The Free Encyclopedia*, 7 March 2022.
- Hoegerl, Rev. Carl. *The Life of Blessed Francis Xavier Seelos, Redemptorist*, Liguori, 2000.
- Kus, Fr. Robert J. "Bl. Francis Xavier Seelos, C.Ss.R." *Saintly Men of Nursing: 100 Amazing Stories*, Red Lantern Press, 2017, pp. 77-79.
- Murray, Fr. John. "The Life of a Roving Redemptorist." Seelos.org.
- "Seelos Health Care." Seelos.org.

14 - Sister Henrietta of Hough, C.S.A.

- "Henrietta, Sister, CSA." *Encyclopedia of Cleveland History.* Cleveland: Case Western Reserve Press, 2022.
- Wolf, Rev. Msgr. Robert C. *Henrietta of Hough: She reclaimed a Cleveland slum*, 1990.

15 - Blessed James Miller, F.S.C.

- "Blessed James Miller." *LaSalle.org*, 2019.
- Contributors to Wikipedia. "James Miller (religious brother)." *Wikipedia: The Free Encyclopedia*, 24 May 2022.
- Ehrlick, Darrell. "Martyr, SMU grad a candidate for Roman Catholic sainthood." *Winona Daily News*, retrieved February 11, 2018.
- Mayorga, Aaron. "Murder of a Lasallian educator: Remembering Brother James Santiago Miller." *The Quadrangle*. Retrieved February 11, 2018.

16 - Ms. Jean Donovan

- Carrigan, Ann. *Salvador witness: The life and death of Jean Donovan*. Orbis Books, 2005.
- Contributors to Wikipedia. "Jean Donovan." *Wikipedia: The Free Encyclopedia*, 20 November 2021.
- [Film] - *Roses in December*. 1982.

17 - Blessed Joseph Gerard, O.M.I.

- Contributors to Wikipedia. "Joseph Gérard." *Wikipedia: The Free Encyclopedia*, 25 March 2022.
- "Bd. Joseph Gerard." *Butler's Lives of the Saints: New Full Edition: May*, Revised by David Hugh Farmer. Burns & Oates/The Liturgical press, 1996, p. 166.
- "Blessed Joseph Gérard Missionary of Lesotho." OMI Postulation.ENG, no date.
- O'Hara, Gerard. *Father Joseph Gérard: Oblate of Mary Immaculate*. 1988.

18 - Saint Juan Diego

- Amadio, Michael. *Nican Mopohua: The chronicles of the Marian apparition of Our Lady of Guadalupe, the canonization of St. Juan Diego, and devotions and prayers*. Lulu.com, 2021.
- Chávez, Eduardo. *Our Lady of Guadalupe and Saint Juan Diego: The historical evidence (Celebrating faith: Explorations in Latino spirituality and theology)*. Rowman & Littlefield Publishers, 2006.

- Contributors to Wikipedia. "Juan Diego." *Wikipedia: The Free Encyclopedia*, 9 June 2022.
- Editors of Encyclopedia Britannica. "St. Juan Diego: Mexican saint." 1 Jan 2021.
- Saunders, Fr. William. "Saint Juan Diego and Our Lady," *Arlington Catholic Herald* reprinted in catholiceducation.org, 2004.

19 - Saint Ignatius of Loyola, S.J.

- "St. Ignatius of Loyola." *Butler's Lives of the Saints: New Full Edition: July*, Revised by Peter Doyle. Burns & Oates/The Liturgical press, 1999, pp. 248-259.
- Contributors to Wikipedia. "Ignatius of Loyola." *Wikipedia: The Free Encyclopedia*, 19 June 2022.
- Edward A. Ryan. "St. Ignatius of Loyola: Spanish saint." *Britannica*, 1 January 2021.
- Sklar, Peggy A. *St. Ignatius of Loyola: In God's service.* Paulist Press, 2001.

20 - Sister Ita Ford, M.M.

- Contributors to Wikipedia. "Ita Ford." *Wikipedia: The Free Encyclopedia*, 14 June 2022.
- Evans, Jeanne. *Here I am, Lord: The letters and writings of Ita Ford.* Orbis Books, October 2005.
- Noone, Judith. *The same fate as the poor.* Orbis Books, May 1996.
- O'Boyle, John. *Martyrs of El Salvador: Their tapes and letters.* 2011.
- Swedish, Margaret. *A message too precious to be silenced: The four U.S. church women and the meaning of martyrdom*, January 1992.
- Zagano, Phyllis. *Ita Ford: Missionary martyr.* Paulist Press: January 1996.

21 - Saint Madeleine-Sophie Barat, R.S.C.J.

- Ball, Ann. "Saint Madeleine Sophie Barat (1779-1865)." *Modern saints: their lives and faces, Book Two*, pp. 93-100. TAN Books: 1990.
- Contributors to Wikipedia. "Madeleine Sophie Barat." *Wikipedia: The Free Encyclopedia*, 14 June 2022.
- Kilroy, Phil. *Madeleine Sophie Barat: A life.* Paulist Press, 2000.

- "St. Madeleine Sophie Barat." *Butler's Lives of the Saints: New Full Edition: May*, Revised by David Hugh Farmer. Burns & Oates/The Liturgical Press, 1996, pp. 141-143.

22 - Saint Marianne Cope, O.S.F.

- Ball, Ann. "Mother Marianne of Molokai, O.S.F. (1838-1918)," pp. 287-293. *Modern saints: their lives and faces.* TAN Books: 1990.
- Contributors to Wikipedia. "Marianne Cope." *Wikipedia: The Free Encyclopedia*, 14 June 2022.
- Gangloff, Sr. Mary Francis OSF. *The life and legacy of Saint Marianne Cope, OSF*, 2013.
- Hanley, Sr. Mary Laurence & Bushnell, O.A. *Pilgrimage & exile: Mother Marianne of Molokai*, Manual Publishing, November 2009.
- Rigney, Melanie. "Marianne Cope: Providing care with courage. *Radical saints: 21 women for the 21st century.* Franciscan Media: 2020.

23 - Mother Mary Joseph Rogers, M.M.

- Contributors to Wikipedia. "Mary Joseph Rogers." *Wikipedia: The Free Encyclopedia*, 19 June 2022.
- LaVerdiere, MM, Claudette. *On the threshold of the future: The life and spirituality of Mother Mary Joseph Rogers, founder of the Maryknoll Sisters.* Orbis Books, 2011.
- Lernoux, Penny, Jones, Arthur, and Ellsberg, Robert. *Hearts on fire: The story of the Maryknoll Sisters.* Orbis Books, 1993, 2005.

24 - Saint Mary MacKillop, S.O.S.J.

- Barr, Helen. *Veil of miracles: Chiara's journey entwined with St. Mary of the Cross MacKillop*, 2018.
- "Bd. Mary MacKillop." *Butler's Lives of the Saints: New Full Edition: August*, Revised by John Cumming. Burns & Oates/The Liturgical press, 1998, pp. 70-72
- Cadwallader, Alan (Ed.). *In the land of larks and heroes: Australian reflections on S. Mary MacKillop*, 2010.
- Contributors to Wikipedia. "Mary MacKillop." *Wikipedia: The Free Encyclopedia*, 21 June 2022.
- Rigney, Melanie. "Mary MacKillop: Pursuing God's plan despite roadblocks." *Radical saints: 21 women for the 21st century.* Franciscan Media, 2020.

25 - Sister Mary Mercy Hirschboeck, M.M.

- Contributors to Wikipedia. "Elizabeth Hirschboeck." *Wikipedia: The Free Encyclopedia*, 13 June 2022.
- Lernoux, Penny, Arthur Jones, and Robert Ellsberg. *Hearts on fire: The story of the Maryknoll Sisters.* Orbis Books, 1993, 2005.
- "Mary Mercy Hirschboeck, 83, Maryknoll Sister and Doctor," *New York Times*, October 2, 1986, Section B, p. 7.
- "Sister Mary Mercy Hirschboeck, MM." Maryknoll Mission Archives, 2021.

26. - Sister Maura Clarke, M.M.

- Contributors to Wikipedia. "Maura Clarke." *Wikipedia: The Free Encyclopedia*, 14 June 2022.
- Lernoux, Penny, Jones, Arthur, and Ellsberg, Robert. *Hearts on fire: The story of the Maryknoll Sisters.* Orbis Books, 1993, 2005.
- Markey, Eileen. *A radical faith: The assassination of Sister Maura*, Nation Books, 2016.
- Noone, MM, Judith M. *The same fate as the poor.* Orbis Books, 1995.
- "Sister Maura Clarke, M.M." Maryknoll Mission Archives, 2021.

27. - Saint Maximilian Kolbe, O.F.M., Conv.

- Contributors to Wikipedia. "Maximilian Kolbe." *Wikipedia: The Free Encyclopedia*, 23 June 2022.
- Frossard, André. *"Forget not love": The passion of Maximilian Kolbe.* Ignatius Press, 1991.
- LeMay, William. *The life of St. Maximilian Kolbe: Apostle of mass communications.* Independently published, 2019.
- Romb, Anselm. *The Kolbe reader: The writings of St. Maximilian M. Kolbe, OFM Conv.*, Marytown Press, 2007.
- Smith, Fr. Jeremiah J. *The Knight of the Immaculate: Father Maximilian Kolbe.* Pickle Partners Publishing, 2016.
- Stone, Elaine Murray. *Maximilian Kolbe: Saint of Auschwitz.* Paulist Press, 1997.
- Treece, Patricia. *A man for others: Maximilian Kolbe the "Saint of Auschwitz."* Marytown Press, 1993.

28. - Saint Noel Chabanel, S.J.

- Ambroisie, Peter. "Dec 26 – St. Noel Chabanel, SJ, (1613-1649): Priest & martyr, 'Resist your temptation to put down your cross," soul-candy.info, February 21, 2016.
- Contributors to Wikipedia. "Noel Chabanel." *Wikipedia: The Free Encyclopedia*, 26 February 2022.
- Wynne, John J. S.J. *The Jesuit martyrs of North America.* Saint Gregory Press, 1925, 2020.

29. - Saint Paulina of the Agonizing Heart of Jesus, C.I.I.C.

- Contributors to Wikipedia. "Pauline of the Agonizing Heart of Jesus." *Wikipedia: The Free Encyclopedia*, 6 February 2022.
- Farace, Frederick A. *Love's harvest: The life of Blessed Pauline.* Faith Publishing Co., 1994.
- Gannon, Megan C. *Special saints for special people: Stories of saints with disabilities.* Twenty-Third Publications, 2019.
- Vatican.va. "Paulina Do Coracao Agonizante de Jesus." Official Vatican Biography. No date.

30. - Saint Rose Philippine Duchesne, R.S.C.J.

- Ball, Ann. "Blessed Philippine Duchesne, R.S.C.J." *Modern saints: their lives and faces, Book One,* pp. 6-11). TAN Books, 1983.
- Contributors to Wikipedia. "Rose Philippine Duchesne." *Wikipedia: The Free Encyclopedia,* 19 June 2022.
- Cummings, Kathleen Sprows. *A saint of our own: How the quest for a holy hero helped Catholics become American.* The University of North Carolina Press, 2019.
- Mooney, Catherine M. *Philippine Duchesne: A woman with the poor.* Wipf & Stock Publishers, 2007.
- Osiek, Carolyn RSCJ. *Saint Rose Philippine Duchesne: A heart on fire across frontiers.* Society of the Sacred Heart, 2017.

31. Blessed Stanley Rother

- *An ordinary martyr: The life and death of Blessed Stanley Rother* [film], Lampstand, 2018.
- Bond, Susan Rother. *Blessed Stanley Rother: An extraordinary ordinary life.* Bonds Between Us Publishing, 2018. (Children's Book)
- Contributors to Wikipedia. "Stanley Rother." *Wikipedia: The Free Encyclopedia*, 14 June 2022.
- *Fr. Stanley Rother: Biography* [film]. Coronation Media, 2017.
- Ruiz Scaperlanda, María. *The shepherd who didn't run: Fr. Stanley Rother, martyr from Oklahoma.* Our Sunday Visitor Press, 2015.

32. - Saint Teresa of Calcutta, M.C.

- Contributors to Wikipedia. "Mother Teresa." *Wikipedia: The Free Encyclopedia*, 23 June 2022.
- Rigney, Melanie. "Teresa of Calcutta: Loving the unlovable." *Radical saints; 21 women for the 21st century.* Franciscan Media, 2020.
- Ruszala, Michael J. and North, Wyatt. *Mother Teresa of Calcutta: A witness to love.* Wyatt North Publishing, 2015.
- Teresa, Mother and Kolodiejchuk, Brian. *Mother Teresa: Come be my light: The private writings of the Saint of Calcutta.* Doubleday, 2007.

33. - Saint Therese of the Child Jesus, O.C.D.

- Ball, Ann. "Saint Therese of the Child Jesus, O.C.D. – 'The Little Flower' (1873-1897)." *Modern saints: their lives and faces*, pp. 222-237. TAN: 1990.
- Clarke, John & St. Therese of Lisieux. *The letters of St. Therese of Lisieux, Vol 1: 1877-1890*, Institute of Carmelite Studies, 1982.
- Contributors to Wikipedia. "Thérèse of Lisieux." *Wikipedia: The Free Encyclopedia*, 15 June 2022.
- "St. Therese of Lisieux." *Butler's Lives of the Saints: New Full Edition: October*, Revised by Peter Boyle. Burns & Oates/The Liturgical press, 1997, pp. 1-5.
- Therese of Lisieux. *The story of a soul: The autobiography of St. Therese of Lisieux.* Tan Books, 2010.

34. - Servant of God Thomas Frederick Price, M.M.

- Byrne, Patrick James. *Father Price of Maryknoll: A short sketch of the life of Reverend Thomas Frederick Price, Missioner in North Carolina, co-founder of Maryknoll, missioner in China.* Franklin Classics, 2018.
- Contributors to Wikipedia. "Thomas Frederick Price." *Wikipedia: The Free Encyclopedia*, 13 September 2021.
- Hanlon, Kevin, M.M. "Father Price: 'The holy priest.'" *Maryknoll Magazine, September 2019.*
- Murrett, John C. *Tar Heel Apostle: Thomas Frederick Price, Cofounder of Maryknoll*, September 2020. (antiquarian book)

35. - Servant of God Vincent Robert Capodanno, M.M.

- Archdiocese for the Military Services, USA. *Father Capodanno Biography.* No date.
- Contributors to Wikipedia. "Vincent R. Capodanno." *Wikipedia: The Free Encyclopedia*, 30 May 2022.
- DiGiovanni, Stephen M. *Armed with faith: The life of Father Vincent R. Capodanno, M.M.* Independently published, 2018.
- Mode, Daniel. "Vincent Capodanno: The grunt padre, 50 years later." *Maryknoll Magazine*, Sept. 1, 2017.
- Mode, Daniel L. Fr. *The grunt padre: Father Vincent Robert Capodanno – Vietnam 1966-1967*. CMJ Marian Publishers, 2000.